CAMP
Sunset

SAWTOOTH NATIONAL
RECREATION AREA, IDAHO

CAMP
Sunset

A MODERN CAMPER'S GUIDE TO THE GREAT OUTDOORS

Edited by Elaine Johnson and the Editors of *Sunset*

with Matt Jaffe

Oxmoor
House®

Published by Oxmoor House, an imprint of Time Inc. Books
225 Liberty Street, New York, NY 10281

Sunset is a registered trademark of Sunset Publishing Corporation.

WRITERS Matt Jaffe, Paige Russell
EDITORS Elaine Johnson, Betty Wong
CREATIVE DIRECTOR Maili Holiman
DESIGNER Christy Sheppard Knell
PRODUCTION MANAGER Linda M. Bouchard
PRINCIPAL PHOTOGRAPHER Thomas J. Story
PHOTO EDITOR Susan B. Smith
COPY EDITOR Tam Putnam
ASSOCIATE DESIGNER Allison Chi
IMAGING SPECIALIST E. Spencer Toy
EDITORIAL ASSISTANT Nicole Fisher
ASSISTANT PROJECT EDITOR Melissa Brown
ASSISTANT PRODUCTION DIRECTOR Susan Chodakiewicz
PROOFREADER Denise Griffiths
INDEXER Ken DellaPenta

For additional acknowledgments and credits, see page 233.

ISBN-13: 978-0-8487-4708-4
ISBN-10: 0-8487-4708-9

Library of Congress Control Number: 2016931557

Printed in the United States of America

10 9 8 7 6 5 4 3 2 1

First Printing 2016

Time Inc. Books products may be purchased for business or promotional use. For information on bulk
purchases, please contact Christi Crowley in the Special Sales Department at (845) 895-9858.

We welcome your comments and suggestions about Time Inc. Books.
Please write to us at:
Time Inc. Books
Attention: Book Editors
P.O. Box 62310
Tampa, Florida 33662-2310

CONTENTS

— *Preface* —

COME CAMPING WITH *SUNSET!*

A couple of summers back, the editors of *Sunset* magazine in California held a contest for a camping weekend, inviting our readers to tell us why they'd like to join us.

Entries arrived in an avalanche. Some were from newbies, like the woman who had requested a camp stove for her 50th birthday but wasn't sure how to turn it on. A Cub Scout den leader admitted to "an aversion to camping." One reader had decorated her entire family room in a glamping theme, but had yet to venture on a real camping trip. Young parents told us how the arrival of children made them fear their camping days were over. And then there were "mixed" couples—one who felt happy and confident in the outdoors after growing up as a camper; the other who wouldn't venture beyond resorts. Could we help them find common ground?

Eventually we chose two families, all excellent sports, and they headed to Big Basin Redwoods National Park with us for the first-ever Camp Sunset.

Guided by our editors—12 of us, including me—plus some invited experts, the families (see more on page 233) set out to get over their hesitancy about camping and to learn the skills the modern camper needs to know. Together we worked on the tried-and-true: pitching tents, building fires, singing songs, and making s'mores. And we explored the cutting edge—how to make camping comfortable and even pretty, how to shake cocktails and bake chocolate cake in a dutch oven. For extra fun, our campers earned merit badges for their efforts.

As you can imagine, we had a blast. But who knew that the trip would be just the beginning? As the weekend drew to a close, our campers shyly admitted that they had learned a ton but still needed much more on the basics. And back at the office, the avalanche of contest entries remained from other would-be campers. We wished we could have taken every one of them on the trip.

More than anything, their entries spoke to a longing for the deep connection of time spent in nature. Even non-campers seemed to understand that a sojourn outdoors nurtures the soul and brings everyone together. They just didn't know how to get started.

And so we got started on this book.

Camping DNA

Since *Sunset*'s founding in 1898, exploring the West's wild places has been part of our bread and butter (or hash balls and bacon grease, going by our 1901 story titled "Practical Hints on Camp Cooking"). Stories and books over the years have mirrored innovations in camping gear, not to mention refinements in camp cuisine.

In a 1917 story, we praised options for comfortable car camping, especially "a camp-body made for your car" (the first RVs were introduced in Los Angeles in 1910). "It resembles closely an undertaker's wagon, but only in appearance. It can be fitted to a chassis by any good wagon-builder in an hour." Stories about new camping equipment like gasoline stoves came out around the same time.

Our first camp cookbook, *Sunset's Grubstake Cookbook*, debuted in 1934, with charming but brief advice for adventuring and creating recipes for stews, pancakes, and the like.

By 1959, we'd raised the standards for food; our story "The Art of Camp Cookery" included directions for roasting bacon and just-caught trout on a stick, and baking mincemeat–port wine pie in a dutch oven.

Glamorous camping, or "glamping," was a newly coined term in 2008. "Problem: Love the outdoors, hate camping. Solution: Swap your sleeping bag for a feather bed," our May magazine cover story promised. Readers took to the concept like blue jays to pancake crumbs.

Since then, we've published near-yearly features on the best campgrounds, gear, and four-star recipes; in 2014, we included a chapter of adventurous camping recipes in *The Great Outdoors Cookbook* (Oxmoor House).

A new book for a new era

As we discovered at our Camp Sunset weekend, it was time for a camping book that brought together our years of advice into one handy, beginner-friendly volume. In keeping with the modern era, you'll find loads of complementary resources on *sunset.com/ campsunset*, including last-minute campsites, guides to the national parks, our favorite deluxe RV trailers, and how-to camping videos.

Go ahead, come camping with *Sunset*. We guarantee you'll have the time of your life along the way.

Elaine Johnson

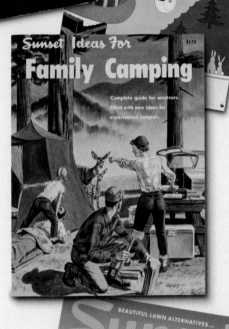

— Introduction —

IT'S THE STARS THAT GET YOU FIRST. After the campfire dies down and the sweet confection of a s'more is just a remembrance on your tongue, your eyes adjust to the darkness, and the arching reach of the heavens is revealed as if for the first time. You stand agape, marveling. And should something wake you in the wee hours, you'll find the twinkling even brighter, the black background blacker, the Milky Way attendant. These are not the stars of home, few and pale.

The great joy of camping is not that you get to spend the night in a tent, but that camping sweeps away the layers between you and what's most natural, which is you, in nature. That's why it doesn't matter if you're sleeping in a platform tent with duvets and turndown service or on the ground in a wispy backpacking shelter. "Camping" covers a huge spectrum, from dehydrated astronaut food to catered repasts, from the remote Alaska tundra of Denali National Park to the miles of sand at Half Moon Bay less than an hour from San Francisco. No matter your style or location, the point is to watch time slow down, to feel your body align itself with the rhythms of the universe. To be in the clear, clean air so long that you forget to marvel at how clear and clean it is.

Camping happily reduces life to its most elemental needs—food and shelter and the occasional dose of medicinal dark chocolate—leaving long stretches where you can simply think. Or observe. Or do nothing.

Whether you're a first-time camper, a day-hiker, kayaker, or just someone who likes to stretch out in a hammock by a lake, we hope you'll use this guide with its essential skills, activity ideas, tips, and recipes as your launchpad to unforgettable outdoor adventures.

SAMUEL P. TAYLOR STATE
PARK, CALIFORNIA

CHAPTER 1

Getting ORGANIZED

The best thing about camping is spending time someplace so beautiful it takes your breath, and your worries, away. We know not everybody agrees. We know some people look at camping the way they look at kale: as a thing they're supposed to like but suspect they won't. But we believe that a good camping trip is the most fun you can possibly have. IT JUST TAKES A LITTLE PLANNING TO MAKE SURE YOU HAVE A MADE-TO-ORDER TRIP, perfect for your camping personality, at a place you're sure to love.

— Choosing a —

CAMPGROUND

When picking a campground, nothing beats friends' personal recommendations, especially if they recently stayed at a particular spot. In addition to deciding whether you want to rough it in a primitive campground or go for the comparative comfort of a developed one (see page 14), keep the following questions in mind.

TUOLUMNE MEADOWS,
YOSEMITE NATIONAL PARK

WHAT ARE THE AMENITIES?

Especially if you're new to camping, it's helpful to choose a campground with such services as a general store, ice and firewood, and laundry facilities. And if flush toilets and hot showers are a priority, check the website to confirm what you'll find at the location.

WHAT CAN YOU DO?

If you want to hike, mountain bike, or kayak, look for campgrounds with trails and water access. It's nice to keep your vehicle parked and explore straight out of the campground, or to have only a short drive to your outings.

HOW CROWDED IS IT?

Larger campgrounds, almost by definition, are busier because more people are coming and going. If you're noise sensitive, pay attention to the campground's proximity to roads and railroad tracks. There are some gorgeous coastal campgrounds in Southern California, for example, that get shaken every few hours by rumbling freight trains. Many campgrounds have online maps that show the overall location, and also the layout and proximity of campsites to one another.

WHAT TYPE *of* CAMPER ARE YOU?

CANYONLANDS
NATIONAL PARK, UTAH

FIRST-TIMER

You want to be wowed with big views, yes, but not until you've had a hot shower. Look for developed campgrounds with amenities (page 14). You might also consider sites that are just a short drive away from town. After all, this is vacation, right?

FAMILY

No way you're packing all that gear unless you have a site reserved where there's more to do than ("borrring!") stare at the trees. Think skin-tingling swims, fishing with bamboo poles, and easy hiking at campsites with nearby lakes or beaches. Check out tips for "Camping with Kids" (page 21).

ADVENTURER

Kicking back in a camp chair is no vacation. You're looking for an adrenaline rush—and are not afraid to sweat for it. Consider primitive sites, and look for places from which you can explore backcountry or ponder the possibilities of peak scrambles, canoeing, or whitewater rafting.

SPONTANEOUS

You're not so great with the months-in-advance reservations, but camping this weekend sure sounds good. If you don't have a campsite reservation, shoot for a first-come, first-served site and check our tips for last-minute campers (page 25).

— *Types of* —
CAMPGROUNDS

DEVELOPED

Designed for car camping (see page 20), many developed campgrounds at national and state parks offer basic creature comforts like bathrooms, showers, and potable water. The campsites are usually assigned spaces that include picnic tables and fire rings or grills. You can make reservations for many of these campgrounds (see page 25), which is a necessity in popular parks. Developed campgrounds vary widely, from those with sensitively placed sites that blend into the environment to some where the experience is more like pitching a tent in a parking lot.

PRIMITIVE

Exactly what a primitive campground offers depends on the agency that administers it. Some primitive campgrounds have vehicle access and simple pit toilets, but no tap water or showers. Others require a hike to the site. Most of these areas are first-come, first-served, but do your homework as, surprisingly enough, many do require reservations or permits.

GROUP

Usually separate from main campgrounds, these sites are open only by reservation to large groups. The sites may be either developed or primitive.

GRAND CANYON
NATIONAL PARK

JOSHUA TREE NATIONAL
PARK, CALIFORNIA

CAMPING
— in the —
DESERT

When camping in the desert, what you lose in forests and mountain lakes you gain in epic landscapes and starry skies splashed by the Milky Way. The desert makes it easier to get away from it all. And as a bonus, consider this: no bugs.

The desert is far more diverse than most people expect, with considerable variation in vegetation and topography. In the western U.S. alone, there are four distinct systems —the Chihuahuan, Great Basin, Mojave, and Sonoran—as well as separate subregions, like the Colorado Desert in southeast California. Though notorious for heat, deserts are actually defined by their lack of rainfall, averaging less than 10 inches per year.

The basic rules of camping apply in the desert, but keep in mind a few particulars.

Stay in an established campground first
If you've never camped in the desert, try a campground with facilities, especially running water, in a state or national park.

Bring extra water
Except in developed campgrounds, water will be scarce. Combined with low humidity, that can lead to dehydration, and you'll need to bring about 2 gallons of water per person per day. It's also important to replenish minerals in the bloodstream so pack sports beverage powders with electrolytes, and have salty snacks, like peanuts, on hand.

Keep your gas tank full
It's a long way between gas stations, even on interstates. Make sure you've recently serviced your car, particularly if you expect to travel off paved roads.

Create shade
While you can try to find a spot up against the boulders or underneath an alcove, desert shade is in short supply. So bring several tarps and some rope to create your own sun protection over the kitchen area and tents.

Prepare for wind
Desert wind storms are common. That means you'll need to stabilize your tent so it doesn't collapse or blow away. Look for sites where shrubs or boulders can serve as a windbreak. Some people tie the tent with rope to large rocks for greater stability, while others collapse their tents during the day by disconnecting poles from the base, then weighting the tent in place.

Take along sand stakes
The combination of wind and loose soil means that stakes easily get loosened, reducing tent stability. Stakes designed specifically for sand (or snow) will better anchor the tent. Keep tent zippers clear, as fine sand is their mortal enemy. Take along a simple zipper-care kit consisting of a brush to clean the teeth and a lubricant such as an oil spray like WD-40.

Dress for sun
Lightweight, light-colored, and loose-fitting clothing is ideal for sunny, hot conditions. Items with UV protection offer a bonus.

Get ready for cold nights
With little cloud cover to keep warmth in, deserts can get quite chilly at night. Bring some layers to throw on after the sun goes down. Snow is not uncommon in high deserts during winter.

Be mindful of the critters
While bears are unlikely (see page 164), rattlesnakes and scorpions are present in many areas. Never reach into gaps between boulders where snakes may nestle, and shake out your shoes in case scorpions have crawled inside.

Protect cryptobiotic soil crust
Actually a layer of biotic organisms, including algae, mosses, and lichens, this ground cover is a kind of living dirt. Watch out for any raised, lumpy soils, and never walk on or pitch your tent on cryptobiotic crust.

CAMPING
— at the —
BEACH

Go ahead, spend hundreds on a room at a posh resort. Or pay twenty bucks to camp at the beach, where you'll wake up to the sound of the surf for a fraction of the price.

Surfers have been sleeping at the beach (legally and illegally) for generations, and there's no denying the romance of spending the night along the coast. Just remember that beach camping poses a few extra challenges.

Know what to expect
Not all beach camping is literally on the beach. Many, if not most, beach campgrounds—particularly those near shorebird nesting spots—are set a short distance back from the sand. The trade-off is that sites on bluffs or tucked in the forest will offer more protection. Beach campgrounds with reservations fill up quickly, so check to find out how early you can nail down your spot. And unless specifically permitted, don't set up in the fragile dune habitat.

Holding your own
Skip standard tent stakes (see page 29) and go with snow or sand stakes to provide more grip. For an even stronger hold, fill sacks or plastic garbage bags with sand. Attach guy lines to them, then dig holes a couple of feet farther than you normally would and bury the bags to more firmly anchor the tent.

Pay attention to tides
Set up well above the mean high-tide line. A promising spot at low tide could be submerged when the tide rolls in, or even get swamped by a large wave. You don't want that: You're camping, not house-boating.

Protect thyself
The beach is actually a harsher environment than you might expect. You're exposed to the elements, so stay hydrated and keep yourself covered to avoid sunburn. Lightweight, loose-fitting clothing and hats are essential.

Set up a shade structure
The golden age of the golden tan is long past. You'll want to take cover periodically, and because tents can turn into broilers during the day, a simple, collapsible shade structure gives you a place to escape the sun. Polyurethane-coated nylon is better than siliconized nylon, which sand mercilessly sticks to.

Manage the sand
Inevitably, you'll fight a mostly losing battle against sand. But a doormat to wipe off your feet and a whisk broom to sweep out the tent will give you a fighting chance. If you plan to do a lot of beach camping, consider getting a tent that lets you zip mesh windows closed to limit sand intrusion.

Put up the rain fly at night
A foggy night will mean a soaked tent, so use the rain fly. And cover towels and anything else you want to leave out with a tarp.

JULIA PFEIFFER BURNS
STATE PARK, CALIFORNIA

CAR CAMPING

It doesn't mean that you literally sleep in your car, although that's sometimes an option. Instead, car camping refers to packing up a vehicle, then driving to a campground and unloading gear, usually without having to walk any great distances. Car camping can include both developed and primitive campsites.

DISPERSED CAMPING

On select public lands, you can camp pretty much anywhere you want for free. Some agencies prohibit dispersed camping within a mile of established campgrounds and near watering holes used by wildlife. To minimize environmental impact, campers are also encouraged to use an existing campsite rather than create their own. The freedom of dispersed camping comes with additional responsibilities, because you won't find any facilities and will have to pack out all your trash.

BACKCOUNTRY or WILDERNESS CAMPING

Kiss those wheels goodbye and head out on foot, by canoe, or on horseback to boldly go where no RV has gone before. Because you'll do your own hauling, gear weight becomes a critical concern. Depending on the availability of a source that can be safely filtered, you may have to bring in your own water. Some wilderness camping takes place at remote designated campsites with simple amenities, such as fire rings, but typically do not have toilets or water.

WHAT IS

Glamping?

Glamping *(aka "glamour camping") is for people who don't want to haul in and set up their own gear. It often means staying in furnished yurts or tricked-out safari-style tents, with dining facilities and showers available nearby. Outfitters typically will also do the cooking and cleanup for you. In general, we lean toward being hands-on when we're out in nature, but see our "Glamp It Up" tips (page 38) for easy pointers on making your camping trip more comfortable.*

CAMPING
— with —
KIDS

Get them onboard early
Build up some antici-
pation for camping.
Narrow down the
destinations to those
with swimming or
boating, as well as
amenities like snack
bars (nothing beats ice
cream on a hot day!).
Have the kids help pick
the final destination by
giving them options,
and show photographs
to get them excited.

Go close
Until the family gets
used to camping, you
might want to avoid
a long drive and the
endless and inevitable
"Are we there yets?"
before you've even
started unpacking.

Gear them up
Everybody should
have a day pack in
which to stash a
headlamp, flashlight,
water bottle, or just
favorite stuff from home.
And pack separate
duffels for each kid's
clothing to avoid
confusion.

Plan for fun
Glorious mountain
views may be enough to
keep parents happily
occupied. Not kids. Go
low tech—bring craft
supplies and design
games and activities
such as those in
chapters 4 (page 155)
and 5 (page 195).

Assign tasks
Everyone has to pitch
in, and after some initial
grumbling, most
children will feel good
about helping out with
such jobs as food prep
(page 84), dishwashing,
or wood collecting.

Set some boundaries
Both for your own
peace of mind and
out of respect for
others, make it clear
to the children just
where your campsite's
boundaries are and
what the campground's
rules are for quiet time.

Grab time for yourself
You need to remember
why you're out in
nature too.

HAVE RV,
Will Camp

No pitching a tent. Maybe a kitchen, bathroom, and even satellite TV. Purists might scoff at the thought of camping in an air-conditioned, four-wheel land yacht. But lots of people love their RVs as a comfy alternative to sleeping on the ground. There are many options to either rent or buy, including iconic Airstreams and pop-up campers. Here are a few.

1.

MOTORHOMES

They have beds, kitchens, bathrooms—plus generators and water and waste tanks. But narrow roads are challenging and mileage can be less than 10 mpg.

2.

LIGHTWEIGHT TRAILERS

Most passenger cars can tow these tiny RVs. Teardrop models have a snug sleeping space for two and an open-air kitchen in back. Stand-up trailers sleep up to four, and tent trailers fold out when parked.

3.

CAMPER VANS

Camper vans, including vintage VW vans or luxe Mercedes Sprinters, are comfortable and easy to drive. Most sleep up to four, and have a kitchen and dining table, but no toilet.

4.

FULL-SIZE TRAILERS

Up to 35 feet long, they have kitchens, bathrooms, and sleeping space. To tow one, your vehicle needs a hitch, electrical wiring, and a controller for the trailer's brakes.

— Making —
RESERVATIONS

Camping is a liberating experience, except for having to plan six months ahead of time to snag a site at leading parks—that is, if you're lucky. Unless you're heading into the backcountry or plan to set up on public lands that don't restrict campers to established campgrounds, you'll have to get your act together and be ready to pounce when prime sites first open up.

KNOW HOW BOOKING WORKS

Familiarize yourself with *Recreation.gov*, the booking site for 12 federal agencies (including national parks and forests), and *ReserveAmerica.com*, which handles reservations for thousands of public and private parks around the country. Minutes can count when campsites first open up for reservations, so be logged in and ready to go. Booking online is much faster than over the phone.

MARK YOUR CALENDAR

Know how far in advance you can book a campsite. Many campsites become available six months in advance, meaning that August dates open up on February 1. Some campsite reservations even open a year ahead of time! And watch out for variations: Yosemite National Park, for example, puts up a full month of dates five months in advance, on the 15th of the month. As mentioned, some campgrounds sell out within minutes, so find out what time reservations open.

GO AT LESS CROWDED TIMES

If you're set on a location, consider trying to book during the week, when demand will be lower.

HAVE FAITH

Those with blessed campsite karma swear that it's worth checking for reservations even a few days before you're planning to go, because last-minute cancellations are common.

FIRST-COME, FIRST-SERVED CAMPSITES

Yes, you do need to plan ahead for the most-coveted camping destinations, like Grand Canyon National Park. But with a bit of research, you'll discover that many developed campgrounds in beautiful locations are available on a first-come, first-served basis. The key is to arrive early, especially before summer or holiday weekends. Friday morning is good; Thursday afternoon is even better. You'll have the best luck midweek or off-season.

Some campgrounds in the reservation system also set aside a few sites for walk-ins. For example, believe it or not, Yosemite National Park, where reserved campsites are generally full from April through September, offers first-come, first-served campsites. You can also target campgrounds that don't take any reservations and those that are farther from main roads. In any case, call ahead to the visitor center for a sense of availability and nearby options.

— *Tents* —

GIMME SHELTER

It's amazing how a layer of nylon and a few lengths of flexible aluminum pole are just about all you need for home sweet home in the outdoors. Settle into your tent after a long day of hiking or canoeing, and that thin barrier creates an unmistakable sense of security and privacy. Just keep in mind that the perfect tent for all situations only exists in a marketer's wildest dreams.

LAKE ALPINE, SIERRA NEVADA MOUNTAINS

DOME

The rounded canopy means that these are both stronger and more weather-resistant than other choices. Rain drains and snow slides off the arched roofline more quickly, and dome tents also can better withstand windy conditions. The main drawback is that the sloping roof reduces living space.

CABIN

These have four nearly vertical walls. The shape creates the most living space and peak height of any tent type, and some cabin tents also feature divided areas that are ideal for families. But the upright profile does mean that cabin tents are more vulnerable to wind.

BASIC
Tent Shapes

A-FRAME or RIDGE

These are the classic pup tents of Boy Scout jamborees and old war movies. Easy to set up, A-frames are best for sleeping and simple shelter, but limited peak height and interior space make them a less comfortable spot for hanging out during the day.

TUNNEL/HOOP

This design uses one to three hoops to create a rounded roofline. They have more interior space than A-frames, and smaller hoop tents are popular with backpackers because of their surprising sturdiness and lighter weight, but do require staking. Larger styles can sleep eight or more people.

KEY QUESTIONS TO CONSIDER

How am I actually going to use this tent?

Maybe you have fantasies of channeling your inner Cheryl Strayed and heeding the call of the wild on multi-day backpacking trips. But be honest: If you're likely to be camping within 50 feet of your car, not in the High Sierra on the Pacific Crest Trail, go for comfort and size and don't worry about shaving off a few pounds of unnecessary weight.

How big should my tent be?

When it comes to tents, one size does not fit all. In fact there's no industry-wide standard for how big a two- or three-person tent actually is, meaning that there can be a fine line between close and claustrophobic. And like women's fashions (what exactly is Size 0, anyway?), tent sizes can run small. So a two-person tent will fit two people, with little or no room for gear.

Most people should go up at least one size for basic comfort, or even double the capacity if you'll be sharing the tent with a child or pet. One rule of thumb is to figure that each camper needs 25 square feet, but also pay attention to the geometry, because irregular shapes and slanting walls will cut into living space.

When am I going to go camping?

Try to anticipate when and where you're most likely to pitch your tent. If, for example, you typically camp during summer at lower elevations, there's no point in shelling out the shekels for a hard-core expedition tent rated for use at Everest base camp. When it comes to weather, you'll be looking at four basic choices of tents.
TWO-SEASON These lighter-duty tents work well from late spring into early fall, if not always at higher elevations or during windy and rainy conditions.
THREE-SEASON The most popular camping option, three-season tents (for spring, summer, and fall) provide comfort during moderate weather conditions, with both ample mesh panels for airflow on hot nights and good protection from rain.
EXTENDED-SEASON These are strengthened with additional poles. They can handle light snowfall and mild wintry conditions, but the trade-off is you lose some ventilation panels.

FOUR-SEASON Tough and designed for extreme weather, four-season tents feature a lower profile, durable fabrics, and additional poles to stand up to serious conditions. For all that winter comfort, you lose ventilation in summer and gain extra tent weight.

CONSTRUCTION

DOUBLE WALL VS. SINGLE WALL Most tents are double-walled, meaning that the primary tent and its ventilation openings are protected against weather by a removable rain-fly covering (see Rain Fly opposite). Ultralight single-wall tents use waterproof fabrics that don't require the added protection afforded by a rain fly.
FABRICS Many tents are made of nylon, although there's considerable variation in weight and durability. Tent specs will include a waterproofing rating for rain flies and floors, and you'll want a number that's at least 1,500mm P.U. or higher if you expect lots of rain.
SEAMS Sewn seams keep everything together but also are potentially vulnerable to leaking. Look for tents with seams factory-sealed with tape to close needle holes. Over time, you may need to add a layer of sealant to close small openings.

HOW TO

Shop for a Tent

Shop at an outdoors store with experienced, knowledgeable staff for the best service.

Have a staffer set up the tent so you can get a sense of the ease of use, then lie down inside to see if the size seems right.

Test the zippers. If zippers don't easily track, they are unlikely to work well outside or stand up to heavy use.

Check to see if material is flame-retardant, because embers from fires are an ever-present threat at campgrounds.

POLES Flexible and durable, poles form your tent's skeleton. The more poles, the greater the structural integrity of your tent. Shock-corded poles, with an elastic cord running through the separate segments, are the easiest to use. Many high-end tents use carbon fiber poles, but anodized aluminum alloy is also dependable. Cheaper tents use fiberglass poles, which are heavier and prone to breakage.

STAKES Whether steel, aluminum, or carbon fiber core, stakes handle the hard work of anchoring your tent into the ground. Tents come with stakes, but you can also pick up sets that are better for specific conditions.

COLOR Tent color is about more than making a campground fashion statement. Darker and neutral colors are less obtrusive and dry faster once the sun is out. They block more light, a big plus on hot days, though a drag on overcast ones. Yellow and other brightly colored tents let in a lot more sun, but the risk is you might get too hot and start feeling like a nylon-wrapped baked potato.

OTHER FEATURES

WINDOWS If you're primarily camping in hot conditions, look for the maximum amount of windows to promote airflow. And because conditions change, spend a little extra for windows that have zippered or Velcro closures.

DOORS Unless you're camping solo, look for tents with at least two doors on opposite sides, to eliminate the dreaded middle-of-the-night crawl-over when someone has to get out to the bathroom.

ROOF VENT This opening in the top of the tent promotes circulation and helps release built-up condensation.

BATHTUB FLOOR This will decrease, though not totally eliminate, your chances of sleeping in a puddle. The waterproof base and floor material extends partway up the side of the tent, where it connects to the wall, putting the seams at least several inches above the ground.

RAIN FLY This waterproof cover can be your best buddy when conditions turn soggy or cold. Look for a full-coverage rain fly that fits over your tent's roof and reaches almost to the ground to provide maximum protection.

FOOTPRINT A good way to limit your floor's exposure to rocks, roots, and other jagged items on the ground, a footprint is a custom-fitted ground cloth that matches the tent's exact dimensions and shape. It reduces the threat of water exposure, and creates an added layer of insulation between campers and the ground.

VESTIBULE, POCKETS, AND GEAR LOFTS A vestibule will give you extra protected space for gear and boots and can be either built into the tent design or available as an add-on. Pockets and mesh gear lofts offer other places to store and organize your stuff.

— *Sleeping Gear* —

GET A GOOD NIGHT'S SLEEP

Few aspects of camping have improved as much as your choices for sleeping gear. From cozy sleeping bags to cushy pads and lots more, today's options are all about customizing your experience for maximum comfort.

SLEEPING BAGS

Your sleeping bag is as individual as a caterpillar's cocoon, a personal zone of comfort that's key to how well you'll sleep while camping. While no bag guarantees a perfect night, you'll go a long way by choosing one for the conditions where you tend to camp.

Temperature Ratings

SUMMER BAGS Usually lighter weight and easily packable; good for conditions 30° and higher.
THREE-SEASON Designed to handle winter conditions down to around 20°, and incorporating hoods with cinches and other features to hold in warmth.
WINTER BAGS Best in conditions 20° or below, and bulkier thanks to additional insulation. Keep in mind that temperature ratings vary from company to company, so use them as a general guide only. The most scientific way to compare bags across many brands is to check the EN 13537 rating. EN stands for "European Norm," and refers to an official laboratory testing measurement designed to take the guesswork

out of bag selection. Not all U.S.-made bags use the standard, but those that do display a label indicating the bag's upper temperature limit, its comfort range, and its lower temperature limit.

Bag Shapes

MUMMY Sleep like an Egyptian in these bags, designed with wider shoulders and tapered head and foot areas. Warm, packable, and lightweight, mummy bags are preferred by backpackers, and also work well for car camping in cold conditions and at higher elevations.
RECTANGULAR Considerably less restrictive than mummy bags, the rectangular-shaped bag lets you move around more during the night, and works just fine for moderate weather conditions and in large tents. Unzip a rectangular bag, and it will also double as a comforter when you want to spread out.
SEMI-RECTANGULAR/HYBRID Tapering from the shoulders and the hips to a narrow footbox, these bags are a tweener—a compromise, with more room for moving around than mummy bags and more warmth than rectangular bags.

good-quality), the greater the warmth by weight. The primary drawback of down is that, if it gets wet, it takes much longer to dry than synthetic materials. Some bags use down treated with a hydrophobic coating or have a waterproof, breathable shell to increase water resistance.

SYNTHETIC Especially if you're car camping in mild conditions, bags with synthetic fill do the job just fine. These bags are less expensive, easier to clean, and perform much better when wet. They also work for people with down allergies. As for the trade-offs, you'll have a heavier, bulkier bag that won't retain heat as well, or last as long as a down bag.

Other Features

HOOD For cold conditions, an integrated hood in a mummy bag is a huge asset. Or get a detachable one.

DRAFT TUBE Running parallel to the zipper, it's an insulated tube or flap designed to seal in warmth.

DRAFT COLLAR An insulated tube that encloses the empty areas around the neck and shoulders to eliminate drafts and reduce heat seepage.

SHELL A water- and wind-resistant shell will help keep you warmer when the weather turns nasty.

LINER Purchase a separate liner for added warmth and to keep everything cleaner. Washing it is much easier than cleaning your entire bag.

Materials

GOOSE AND DUCK DOWN Down-filled bags are lightweight and compact, giving a better warmth-to-weight ratio. Check the "fill power" for an idea of a bag's warmth: The higher the number (600–700 is considered

---

HOW TO

Buy a Sleeping Bag

Check the loft
Lay out some bags—whether down or synthetic—and compare thickness. It's hardly scientific, but you can get a better idea of a bag's warmth and construction.

Try it on for size
Slip inside to see how much room you have for your usual sleeping positions and for rolling over. But remember, too much space and the bag will be harder to get warm.

Play with the zippers
There's nothing worse than a zipper that snags, trapping you in your bag. Zippers should glide cleanly and be easy to work while you're actually in the bag. And you'll definitely want double-zippers.

Pair up
Try bags together with different sleeping pads to find the best combination for comfort.

SLEEPING PADS

While kids may tolerate—even revel in—sleeping on bare dirt, adult backs tend to protest. And a grown-up who has spent a restless night is not going to be a happy camper.

A quality foam or air pad does wonders, offering cushioning and warmth by separating you from the cold (and occasionally damp) ground. The rate of insulation is measured as the pad's R-Value, with higher numbers referring to greater warmth. Look for a pad a few inches longer than your height to keep your feet from extending onto the ground.

FOAM PADS Made of dense foam with air cells, these are the simplest style of pads. They're lightweight, cheap, and won't absorb water, but don't fold up as well.

AIR MATTRESSES The next best thing to your own bed, air mattresses inflate with portable pumps and are ideal for car camping in moderate conditions. The main drawbacks are greater weight and a lack of insulation.

AIR PADS Inflated manually (get ready to blow) or with an external pump, air pads are lightweight and packable, though vulnerable to rips.

SELF-INFLATING SLEEPING PADS These allow you to save your lungs and simply undo a valve to automatically fill an open-cell foam layer. Though heavier than manually inflating pads, these pack compactly.

MORE SLEEP GEAR

PILLOWS There's an array of camping and travel pillows, including some made with compressible high-quality foam and others with inflatable air cores. Or bring your favorite pillow from home for an extra touch of comfort.

EYESHADES Reduce the chances of an errant flashlight beam suddenly waking you up.

EARPLUGS Not everyone obeys campground etiquette, and the unfamiliar sounds can keep you awake.

COTS If you find it impossible to sleep on the ground, a lightweight folding cot lets you nap in comfort. Some also weigh under 3 pounds.

CAMPING with **DOGS**

Check the rules
Not all campgrounds allow pets, so know before you go. Obey any leash regulations.

Tag them
No one wants to think about a dog getting lost, but with endless temptations, it's easy for your pal to run off. Making sure your dog is microchipped or has updated ID tags offers peace of mind.

Pack a bowl
Have a water dish on hand to limit the chances of your dog opting for stagnant pools when thirsty.

Throw on a bandana
A brightly colored bandana will help catch your eye if the dog goes running into the woods. Plus it's a good look.

Be tick aware
A topical anti-tick treatment before you go is a really good idea. While camping, check your dog for ticks regularly.

Keep your dog close
Even if the campground doesn't require leashes, a free-ranging dog creates all sorts of problems. Scooby vs. Skunky is no contest. Don't allow your dog to chase wildlife or run into other campsites.

Always clean up
Dog poop can sicken wildlife. And stepping in it is no more pleasant in the forest than it is on a sidewalk.

— Types of —
LIGHTING

LANTERNS

Traditionalists love the intensity of lanterns that burn white gas, propane, and butane. These lanterns, however, are also noisy and hot to the touch, a potential problem when you have kids in camp. (Plus, for safety, they can't be used inside tents.) Many campers opt instead for battery-powered LED lanterns (and some are rechargeable). Just remember to bring enough batteries, and bear in mind that cold weather will affect battery performance. Look for non-glare frosted plastic, rubber bases or legs, and a hook for hanging the lantern.

HEADLAMPS

Hands-free and hassle-free, headlamps are a must-have for camping. Once the province of hard-core mountaineers, headlamps today are so inexpensive, small, and convenient that every camper should have one. A simple LED model goes for about $20 and will let you cook, clean, and gather firewood with hands flashlight-free. Look for waterproof ones if you're canoeing or crossing rivers. You'll also want a headlamp that adjusts from a wide beam to a spot beam. For stargazing (page 225), headlamps with a red-light setting keep your eyes adjusted to the darkness but let you maneuver around the campsite.

FLASHLIGHTS

Even with headlamps and lanterns, flashlights still have their place, as a focused light. Find a flashlight that's both lightweight and durable, because drops are inevitable.

TOOLS

AX, HATCHET, OR CAMP SAW

Many parks now strictly limit wood gathering, but if you're able to forage for some or can buy firewood at the campground, you'll want a tool to cut it to size.

DUST PAN AND WHISK BROOM

Keep that tent free of debris. You'll sleep better and the tent will last longer.

FIRST-AID KIT

Assembled kits offer convenience and reduce the chances of forgetting something essential. Always check the kit to make sure it includes everything that your group might need, especially if someone has a medical condition requiring specific treatment.

KNIFE

Bring along a heavy-duty knife for chores around camp, including cutting rope. Multi-tools and Swiss Army knives are versatile and give you peace of mind that you'll be ready for just about anything.

LIGHTWEIGHT HAMMER OR MALLET

For easier pounding in and removal of tent stakes.

SHOVEL AND TROWEL

Lightweight, foldable shovels can come in handy when you have to attend to the fire or dig out a rock where you want to pitch the tent. If you're camping in an area without toilets, you'll need a trowel to dig a cathole for those special times.

— Other —
CAMP COMFORTS

CAMP CHAIRS

Think you're too much of a purist to haul a camp chair into the backcountry? Think again. Some camp chairs feature ultralight poles and a mesh seat, and they pack down small. You may never sit on a log again.

HAMMOCK

Few sensations are as soothing as the gentle swaying of a hammock. Add a nice breeze and a cold beer late in the afternoon and you have the perfect recipe for a rejuvenating nap. (Some campers skip tents entirely, especially in hot weather, and use hammocks instead. A rain fly and mosquito netting increase comfort, as does an under-quilt.) Always check the weight capacity and that the suspension system uses straps greater than 3/4 inch wide to prevent damage to trees. And never suspend your hammock from a dead tree.

SHOWER

You don't fully appreciate the joy of a quick shower until you can't take one. If you're not at a campground with showers, a simple solar shower lets you rinse off. It consists of a durable bag that you leave in the sun to warm the water. Hang the bag above your head and open a shower nozzle attached to a hose to start the flow. Two rules: Find a discreet spot to set up the shower, and turn off the water as soon as possible to avoid waste.

SHADE SHELTER

In areas without tree cover, such as the beach and desert campgrounds, shade shelters can provide sun and wind protection for picnic tables and tents. Shelters made with waterproof material are also a big help when it rains.

POWER SOURCES

First, a caveat: We encourage you to unplug when you're camping. You'll have plenty of time to post, tweet, text, upload, and download upon your return to the "real world." That said, there are green energy sources, from solar-powered gear, batteries, and generators to camp stoves, that can help you power up.

GLAMP

— *It Up* —

Love the sights and sounds of the great outdoors, but can't live without a comfy bed? Relax—your luxury camp experience awaits.

Get off the ground
Purists be damned: You're under no moral obligation to spend the night on the ground. The best way to make camp feel luxurious? An air mattress with built-in pump (use an adapter with your car's power outlet).

Treat your feet
An indoor-outdoor throw rug or a pair of slippers will make you forget your floor is dirt.

Bring comfort touches from home
Wake up to birdsong and mountain views in your own sheets, on your own pillow, under a cozy alpaca throw.

Keep it clean
Use a small whisk broom to sweep out the tent and keep things tidy.

Create mood lighting
When you're ready to hang out in the tent for the evening, there's no need to blind each other with headlamps. To brighten the entire tent, fill a 1-gallon water jug, then strap a headlamp around it to create a softer interior light. Or pick up a Moroccan-style lantern at an import store, and light it with a battery-powered LED votive (never use real candles).

Light your path
There's no need to roam around in the dark looking for your tent and trying to avoid tent stakes. Mark your way with solar-powered garden lights or tent stakes with integrated LED lights.

Set a beautiful table
Want to make even the simplest camp meal feel three-star? Set the table with a cheery tablecloth, some matching enamel-ware dishes, mugs, and a coffee pot, (see the Resource Guide, page 228), and cloth bandanas for napkins. Get ready for compliments from your camping neighbors.

— Camp —
KITCHEN

Sure, you can keep it simple and skip the cooking gear to live on energy bars and PB&J, with an occasional bite of jerky. But picture this: a brisk morning in late autumn, with the smell of fresh coffee, sizzling bacon, and blueberry pancakes wafting over from the campsite next to you. Face it, less isn't always more, so you'll want to put together a good camp kitchen of your own.

CAMP STOVES

Although it's romantic to think that you'll cook every meal over a campfire, a camp stove is a key piece of gear in your outdoor kitchen, especially when you positively absolutely gotta eat something. And soon.

FUEL There are stoves that use liquid fuel such as gas and kerosene, and work well in winter conditions and at higher elevations, and ultra-lightweight alcohol stoves for backpacking trips. But butane and propane canister stoves tend to be the most popular option for car-campers. These stoves are nice and portable and almost as easy to use as the one in your kitchen. Attach the canister directly to the stove valve (or depending on the model, to a connector pipe valve or hose), then fire it up and get cooking. It can be hard to predict just how much fuel you'll go through, so pack an extra canister or two. You can also use a refillable 1-gallon propane tank (sold at RV-supply stores) that will require an adapter and hose.

SIZE For car camping, don't worry too much about weight, and opt for the stove that best meets your cooking needs. Most camping stoves fold into cases, making them easy to transport. Be sure to check the stove's cooking space because some are truly compact, making it difficult to use a big frying pan and a pot.

Many stoves have two-burner units similar in size to the ones on your home stove—and you can use your regular pots and pans with them. If you're going to be cooking for a large group, a freestanding stove with three burners and prep areas offers more versatility.

POWER Manufacturers love to tout how many BTUs (British Thermal Units) the burners put out, as well as the stove's average boiling time. Stoves with burners firing at 20,000 BTUs or more tend to be of higher quality. But as with temperature ratings for tents, sleeping bags, and pads, these measurements offer only a rough guide to performance.

BUILT-IN WINDSCREEN Wind can greatly reduce the efficiency of camp stoves and blow out burners when they're set at a low flame. While you can often position your stove to minimize breezes, an integrated windscreen makes a big difference. Some Coleman stoves feature HyperFlame burners with built-in windscreens.

AUTOMATIC IGNITION The ignition system uses an electric spark to light the gas, so you won't need any matches or a separate igniter.

EASE OF CLEANING When you're buying a stove, look for one with a sealed surface and a removable grate so it's easy to wipe up any spills.

champ of cooking outdoors. Cook over a charcoal or wood fire with one of these short-legged, cast-iron bad boys, and you'll join a tradition that includes the famed trailblazers Lewis and Clark. With a flanged lid that lets you put hot coals on top, and short legs, a camp dutch oven can cook foods from above and below, making it possible to bake such camp favorites as cinnamon rolls (page 94) and also to simmer stews (page 118). Or invert the lid and it can double as a griddle. Just don't backpack with one! For more tips on cooking with a dutch oven, see page 112.

GRILL GRATES While many campsites have charcoal grills or firepits with grates for cooking, you don't want to arrive at a campsite planning to cook steaks only to discover that there isn't a grill. So check before you go, or bring along a portable grill grate. These have folding legs and can be positioned directly over the heat.

MORE KITCHEN ESSENTIALS

COOLERS You'll want to bring two coolers: one for food and a second for drinks. Everyone will open the drink cooler much more frequently, so having separate coolers helps keep food items colder. Look for coolers with ports to make draining melted ice easier. Test the placement of handles to see how easy it will be to carry the cooler—or choose wheeled models. The quality of insulation varies, and better coolers feature a rubber lid gasket to minimize melting. Some coolers are designed with slots for locks to make them bearproof.

KNIVES For most preparation, a chef's knife and paring knife will take care of everything you need to do, but a bread knife can come in handy as well. Be sure to use a case or carefully wrap the knives in dish towels secured tightly with rubber bands. You don't want to risk injury while unloading or packing the gear.

STURDY GRILLING GLOVES This unsung camping hero has saved many a hand from burns.

MIXING BOWLS You'll want several—made of metal or plastic—on hand for food prep and cleaning. Look for collapsible or nesting bowls for ease of packing.

DISHWARE Leave the fine china at home and find an unbreakable set that you don't mind banging around.

COOKWARE

The big question is whether to bring pots and pans from your home kitchen, or buy ones designed especially for outdoor use (either individual pots and pans or a full packaged set). Ones from your home kitchen work well, though can be bulky. Cookware designed for outdoors tends to be lighter weight, and sets are made to nest and stack together. Whichever option you choose, you'll at least want a large skillet (a 12-inch cast-iron skillet is our pan of choice), a small saucepan, and a pot big enough for cooking pasta (it can double as a dishwashing container).

MATERIALS Cast-iron retains heat and distributes it evenly. Yes, it's heavy, but you won't mind after that first bite of pancake. Aluminum is light and conducts heat efficiently, though it's hard to clean if you burn it, and is susceptible to dings. Stainless steel offers greater durability, but typically costs and weighs more than aluminum. Titanium is both strong and lightweight but be prepared to pay more for its superior strength-to-weight ratio.

DUTCH OVENS No piece of cookware is more synonymous with camping than the dutch oven, the heavyweight

CAMP MUGS Covered, insulated mugs are perfect for morning coffee and can be used for cold beverages the rest of the day—though tinware ones add a touch of style. Get a variety of colors and assign each person their own mug to avoid confusion.

WATER CARRIER WITH SPIGOT You want a big but not huge collapsible container (2½ gallons works well) to haul water from potable sources. The spigot will simplify pouring and reduce spillage.

CUTTING BOARD Be kind to your picnic table. There are lightweight camping cutting boards in different sizes, or just bring one from home.

CAMP TABLE Flat surfaces for eating and food prep are at a premium in campgrounds. You can find folding tables that pack down into stuff sacks and weigh as little as 2½ pounds, plus larger ones that support weight up to 100 pounds.

COOKING TOOLS Basics to have on hand include a spatula, wooden spoon, grilling tongs, wine and can openers, measuring cups and spoons, and a wire whisk. After planning your meals, consider whether any will require special implements.

OPTIONAL ITEMS

TEA KETTLE Handy for boiling water when you want to keep your saucepan free.

EXTENDABLE FORKS S'mores. Hot dogs. Need we say more?

UTENSIL ROLL A lightweight way to keep your utensils together, this canvas organizer has individual pockets for knives, forks, and spoons, and can be suspended from a tree for easy access.

PORTABLE SINKS If you're camping with a group, a sink can help speed up dishwashing. Some are multiple nesting bins (see page 83), others are little more than large basins with collapsible nylon sides and steel bases for stability. There are also simple folding designs with two basins—one for cleaning, the other for rinsing.

CAMP KITCHEN A foldable camp kitchen setup, this has a surface for a camp stove and extra workspace, plus shelves and netting to stash supplies and cookware. Some even have sinks.

FRENCH PRESS
A low-tech method well-suited to the outdoors. French press units for camping use insulated, unbreakable carafes rather than glass. They're more difficult to clean, but the effort is worth it.

BATTERY-POWERED MILK FROTHER
A luxury—that is, until you take your first sip of latte.

JAVA
Junkies

POUR-OVER
Even in our era of infinite coffee complexity, the simple pour-over method may still produce the best cup. All you need is a cone and filters. If there are more than a few people, bring a larger cone and a thermos or coffee pot. One cup of grounds and 6 cups of simmering water make 5 good strong cups of coffee (see page 97).

COFFEE GRINDER
Fresh-ground beans vs. pre-ground is no contest, and bringing an easy-to-use hand-cranked burr grinder is worth a few extra ounces, even for backpackers. Just make sure that the grinder is made of stainless steel or another unbreakable material.

GET READY ✓

Checklist

Use this easy timeline to help you get organized.

ONE WEEK BEFORE
- ❏ Designate one corner of your garage the camping corner.
- ❏ Check the checklist (page 50).
- ❏ Borrow or rent any items you don't have.

TWO DAYS BEFORE
- ❏ Start packing your camping gear.
- ❏ Plan meals.
- ❏ Buy groceries.

ONE DAY BEFORE
- ❏ Make ice blocks (see page 46).
- ❏ Pre-prep food.
- ❏ Make sure you have any necessary maps or location information.
- ❏ Check the weather.

DEPARTURE DAY
- ❏ Pack the cooler (page 46).
- ❏ Pack the car (page 49).
- ❏ Include kids' activities.
- ❏ Head out with enough time to reach camp before dark.

Download at Sunset.com/campinglist

— Getting —

READY TO GO

We've all been there: the frantic Thursday-night search for sleeping bags (in the garage?) and the camp stove (didn't we have fuel for this?) for the leave-on-Friday camping trip. So make sure you start planning a week in advance.

MEAL PLANNING

1. Write out a meal-by-meal menu

The real secret to eating well in camp is thinking it through ahead of time. Look through the recipes in chapter 3 (page 79) and decide what you want to make, starting with a special dinner that's doable and just might be a trip highlight, like Pan-Seared New York Steak (page 117). And think simple too—sandwiches for dinner the night you arrive, or chili (page 98), made at home and warmed up in camp. Finally, plan to eat the most perishable foods (seafood, unfrozen meats, delicate produce) early in the trip.

2. Create ingredients lists

Not only will this help you shop, but as you pack, literally check off each cooking item. It will ensure you won't spend the whole drive wondering whether you forgot cumin for the chili. Life's too short for that.

3. Double-check your cooking gear

It doesn't help to pack all of the makings for a dutch oven stew and then forget the dutch oven. Figure out if there are specific cooking items you need for certain meals, like a big pot for pasta, then add them to your gear list. And make sure that the camp stove is in working order.

4. Go shopping

- Buy in small packages, or just bundle up the portions you need.
- Buy meat vacuum-sealed (some butchers offer this service) to prevent leaks, or use resealable plastic bags.
- Choose quick-cooking ingredients, such as rice noodles or couscous.
- Opt for sturdy produce. Cabbage stays fresh longer than lettuce; apples keep better than strawberries.
- Purchase bagged vegetables. Buying them prepped saves time.

5. Prep what you can before leaving

Many of our recipes have steps marked "At Home," such as preparing marinades, baking mixes, and pasta sauces that will save time once you arrive at camp. You can even marinate then freeze meats. They will double as ice blocks until defrosted. Chop bulky fruit, like cantaloupe and pineapple, for easier packing. Greens can also be washed, wrapped in paper towels, and sealed in food containers or resealable plastic bags.

6. Stay flexible

As the Boy Scouts like to say, "Be prepared." Pack extra fuel for the stove and be ready with quick-and-easy choices if the weather turns nasty, or everyone's too tired to wait for something more elaborate.

THE Cooler

Your goal: food that stays cold, organized, dry, and unsquished, with no massive ice melt by day 3. And don't forget that bringing two coolers—one for food and one for drinks—is ideal if you have the space.

1. KEEP EVERYTHING COLD

Make ice blocks
(They last way longer than cubes.) At least 24 hours ahead, stash two to three large (8 by 10 inch) refreezable ice packs, like ones made by Arctic Ice (see the Resource Guide, page 228), in the freezer. Or fill two soft-sided 96-ounce Nalgene canteens three-quarters full with water (to leave room for expansion) and freeze flat.

Pre-chill food and drinks
This helps ice stay cold. Freeze meat in marinades, and pack seafood frozen. They'll act like extra ice in the cooler and keep longer.

2. PACK LIKE A BAG BOY—OR GIRL

Put fragile stuff on top
Think eggs, lettuce, and herbs.

Stash loose items in a plastic tote
This is the spot for yogurts, that spice jar of ketchup, bags of meats and cheeses, and anything you don't want to lose in the ice. Seal the tote with a lid.

Put ice blocks on the bottom of the cooler
Other heavy items, like meats frozen in marinade, and boxes of cut-up fruit, go at the bottom too.

Fill in empty spaces
Dump ice cubes into the cooler to fill in spaces between items.

3. CONSERVE SPACE

Remove excess packaging
Cut an egg carton in half if you need only six eggs. Seal bacon in a plastic bag but leave any cardboard behind. Stash a single cube of butter in a small container if that will be enough. Fill an empty spice jar with ketchup so you don't bring the whole bottle. You get the idea.

Pre-prep produce
Rinse lettuce and herbs, then wrap in paper towels and a plastic bag. Peel and chop bulky fruits like pineapple and melon, cut bell peppers into strips, and package them in containers.

4. KEEP FOOD ORGANIZED AND DRY

Seal meats, cheeses, and eggs in plastic bags
Foods will stay dry even when ice starts to melt a bit. (But be sure these and all highly perishable foods, like mayo, stay very cold.)

Label everything
Containers marked with masking tape and a Sharpie mean the family can help themselves while you hang out in a hammock.

5. KEEP THE COOLER IN THE SHADE

The ice will last twice as long if you set coolers in the shade once you're at the campground.

PACK IT

Kitchen Gear

Assemble a camping box with utensils, matches, a small cutting board, and other necessities. Keep it ready to go so you don't forget basics. Pack all of the kitchen gear in one or two large bins, and pantry staples in a smaller one, so everything is handy when you cook.

- Decant large bottles of liquids such as olive oil into smaller containers (preferably plastic) in portions you'll use on the trip.
- Don't forget salt, a pepper grinder, and a few spices.
- Foil for cooking and plastic bags or containers for leftovers and lunches are also useful.
- Use kitchen towels to cushion pots and pans and any jars; they'll also come in handy for cleanup.

Clothing

Spending time in nature, you and your clothes are bound to get dirty faster than at home (for kids, make that a whole lot faster). Don't worry about having clean outfits for every day of your trip. Most experienced campers find they're happy making shirts, shorts, and pants last several wearings. (For comfort, plan for fresh undergarments and socks for each day.) You might also bring some quick-dry outdoor clothes you can hand-wash in camp. For more on clothing, see the checklist on page 50.

The Car

USE A CHECKLIST AS YOU LOAD. If slightly compulsive, it's the best way to make sure that everything actually makes it into your vehicle.

LAST IN, FIRST OUT. Think about what you'll do first when you arrive at your campsite, and the priority items you'll want access to. For most people, that means the tent and maybe a warm jacket go on top.

EVERYTHING HAS A PLACE. It may take a few outings before your system is perfected, but if you can standardize where you put each item, you'll take the mystery out of both packing and unpacking.

DON'T OVERSTUFF. You may find that you don't have a good spot for odd-shaped items. Consider getting an enclosed roof box to give yourself extra space. And always ask a vital question: Do I really need it?

BEFORE YOU HIT THE ROAD

- Aim to arrive at the campsite at least a few hours before sunset to allow plenty of time for setup.
- Bring two sets of car keys. And have them carried by two people. Because spending hours looking for your keys somewhere on the Bluebird Trail where you think you dropped them is no fun. Nor is realizing that your car is locked with the keys inside, along with the s'mores ingredients.
- Make sure someone knows where you are headed.

HOW — not to — OVERPACK

The dirty secret is that if you're using a roomy vehicle for car camping, you're probably better off overpacking a bit than leaving something behind. That said, keep these questions in mind as you try to be realistic about what you genuinely need and what conditions you're likely to encounter.

How long will I be away?

If you're camping for only a couple of nights, exercise restraint and explore the virtues of packing light. It will be good practice for longer trips.

Can this item do more than one thing?

Specialized items have less value when you're camping. That big warm down coat would be great for about an hour a day, but a fleece jacket that can be worn on its own or layered with other pieces of clothing will serve more than one function.

CAMPING

Checklist

A good campsite needs just a few elements to be fun and livable.
Our advice: Start with a big list and customize it according to what you need for each
outing. If you can keep some of the gear packed together in between trips,
getting ready will go faster the next time.

BASIC GEAR

- [ ] Tent
- [ ] Ground cloth
- [ ] Sleeping bags
- [ ] Sleeping pads
- [ ] Pillows
- [ ] Flashlights or headlamps and extra batteries
- [ ] Lantern
- [ ] Shade/rain shelter or tarp
- [ ] Rope
- [ ] Water carrier with spigot
- [ ] Folding chairs
- [ ] Day pack
- [ ] Water bottles
- [ ] Multi-tool or Swiss Army knife
- [ ] Hammer or mallet
- [ ] Whisk broom and dust pan (for tent)

CLOTHING

- [ ] T-shirts, short- and long-sleeved
- [ ] Shorts
- [ ] Loose-fitting pants (preferably zip-off)

- [ ] Underwear
- [ ] Socks (synthetic or wool)
- [ ] Swimsuit
- [ ] Sneakers
- [ ] Hiking boots
- [ ] In-camp sandals
- [ ] Pullover or zippered fleece
- [ ] Warm jacket
- [ ] Warm hat
- [ ] Gloves
- [ ] Windproof/water-resistant jacket
- [ ] Sun hat
- [ ] Pajamas

TOILETRIES & MISC.

- [ ] Toothbrush and toothpaste
- [ ] Comb
- [ ] Sunscreen
- [ ] Lip protection
- [ ] Bug repellent
- [ ] Towel
- [ ] Quarters for the showers
- [ ] Soap and soap holder
- [ ] Shampoo

- [ ] First-aid kit
- [ ] Sunglasses
- [ ] Prescription medications
- [ ] Feminine products
- [ ] Clothesline and clothespins
- [ ] Sewing kit
- [ ] Duct tape
- [ ] Trowel
- [ ] Extra toilet paper
- [ ] Pet supplies

ACTIVITIES

- [ ] Small board games (such as Apples to Apples)
- [ ] Books and magazines (such as the current issue of *Sunset*!)
- [ ] Camera or phone for taking pictures; charger cable for car
- [ ] Active games, such as wiffle bats and balls, or badminton rackets and birdies

- [ ] Craft supplies
- [ ] Field guides
- [ ] Binoculars
- [ ] Magnifying glass
- [ ] Ruler
- [ ] Maps
- [ ] Compass
- [ ] Trekking poles
- [ ] Space blanket
- [ ] Song book
- [ ] Guidebook

CAMP KITCHEN

- [ ] Plastic tote bins with handles
- [ ] Cooler and ice (for big groups, bring an extra cooler just for drinks)
- [ ] Stove
- [ ] Stove fuel
- [ ] Butane lighter or matches
- [ ] Hot pads
- [ ] Sturdy grilling gloves
- [ ] Folding table (optional)
- [ ] Small serrated knife or paring knife

- [ ] Chef's knife
- [ ] Bread knife
- [ ] Knife guards (or wrap knives in thick towels and secure with rubber bands)
- [ ] Cutting board
- [ ] Kitchen scissors
- [ ] Children's scissors (for kids to help cook)
- [ ] Measuring cups and spoons
- [ ] Wooden spoon
- [ ] Serving spoons
- [ ] Wide metal spatula
- [ ] Corkscrew
- [ ] Can opener
- [ ] Grater
- [ ] Wire whisk
- [ ] Silicone scraper
- [ ] Vegetable peeler
- [ ] Silicone basting brush
- [ ] Stainless steel mixing bowls (small, medium, large)
- [ ] Silverware

- Utensil roll (optional)
- Tea kettle (optional)
- Coffee/tea gear (cone, filters, and thermos, for example)
- Coffee grinder (optional)
- Battery-powered milk frother (optional)
- Large cast-iron skillet
- Saucepans (small and medium)
- Pasta pot
- Camp dutch oven
- Charcoal
- Charcoal chimney and newspaper
- Sturdy grilling tongs
- Portable grill grate (optional)
- Firewood and kindling (if allowed)
- Hatchet/ax
- Colander (collapsible, if available)
- Dishpan or portable sink
- Biodegradable dish soap
- Sponge
- Nylon mesh scrubber
- Dishtowels
- Plastic tablecloth

- Unbreakable plates
- Camp mugs
- Plastic cups
- Bowls
- Extendable forks for fire
- Paper towels
- Heavy-duty foil
- Resealable plastic bags/containers for lunch/ leftovers
- Trash and recycling bags
- Recipes or this book

CAMP FOOD BASICS

In addition to ingredients for recipes, we like to keep these supplies on hand.

- Coffee
- Tea
- Cocoa mix
- Half-and-half
- Milk
- Butter
- Pancake mix
- Eggs
- Oatmeal and granola
- Bacon or sausages
- Fruit (fresh and dried)
- Bagels
- Juice
- Salt and pepper
- Syrup
- Vegetable oil

- Extra-virgin olive oil
- Red wine vinegar or Champagne vinegar
- Bread
- Peanut butter
- Jam
- Cheese
- Salami/cold cuts
- Crackers
- Mustard and mayo
- Pretzels, chips, etc.
- Salsa
- Cookies
- Jerky
- Go bars
- Pasta
- Marinara or pesto
- Parmesan cheese
- Dried herbs and spices
- Fresh herbs
- Vegetables (preferably sturdy ones such as peppers, broccoli, onions)
- Salad greens
- Emergency foods (ramen, miso soup, sardines, etc.)
- Marshmallows, graham crackers, and chocolate for s'mores
- Beer, wine, and/or cocktail supplies

MY CHECKLIST

- _____
- _____
- _____
- _____
- _____
- _____
- _____
- _____

BIG BASIN REDWOODS
STATE PARK, CALIFORNIA

CHAPTER 2

Camp Setup &

BASIC SKILLS

—

Just because you're outdoors, doesn't mean you need to rough it. Now that you've made your great escape, HERE IS WHAT YOU NEED TO KNOW to find a peaceful spot, pitch your tent, build a fire, and ensure your camp is pretty, functional, and environmentally friendly.

— *Pick* —

YOUR SPOT

Location, location, location. Even the finest tent won't mean a whole lot if you are unhappy with your campsite. So when you're car camping and arrive at a first-come, first-served campground, do a little reconnaissance work. Circle the area to get a feel for the campground. See where the bathrooms and water sources are located, and check for any noteworthy views. Spots farthest away from the entrance should be quieter, as are sites along culs-de-sac and off the main road.

NATURAL FEATURES Proximity to a lovely element like a lake, river, or even a dramatic rock outcropping is a boon. It will provide a hypnotic view for lounging adults and a place within sight of camp for kids to play. Just don't set up camp at a precarious spot with drop-offs nearby.

TREE CANOPY Any trees at your site are good, but if they're oriented to allow morning sun and afternoon shade, so much the better. A site with southern or eastern exposure is great when contending with cold.

ADEQUATE SPACE Figure out how much room you need to comfortably spread out your camp setup and choose the space to match.

PARKING Close by, with an extra spot or two for visiting friends, if that's on the agenda.

CAMPFIRE AREA It should be free of flammable debris and low overhanging branches.

GOOD GROUND Find the flattest possible spot for your tent (you can even put a ball down and see if it starts rolling), ideally on high ground, so you don't wake up in a cold-air pocket and so that rain (if any!) rolls away. Check for rocks, roots, and branches that could disturb sleep, and for depressions in the ground where rain could potentially pool.

A BIT OF PRIVACY You'll want some isolation from other campsites so you don't have to worry about their noisemaking (or yours).

RESTROOMS They're near—but not too near. Being close to the bathroom might seem like a plus, but it also means increased activity and noise throughout the night. You might also want to find a spot upwind from the facilities.

WATER SOURCE The water spigot is also a hub of campground activity. Establishing camp a distance away will spare you foot traffic but make hauling water a bit more difficult.

HAZARDS TO AVOID

DEAD TREES Look around the campsite and take note of standing dead trees, especially those with hanging limbs that could come down. Even living trees can have dead limbs that might fall.

LOOSE ROCKS Avoid setting up camp at the base of cliffs or slopes where loose rocks and other debris have collected. There's more where that came from.

LOW-LYING AREAS Avoid these—if it rains, you've put yourself right in the path of water flow and where puddles form.

STAGNANT POOLS To minimize mosquitoes, choose dry, sunny areas that have some exposure to breezes.

WILDLIFE Check to see if the campsite sits near any wildlife trails (look for narrow bands of tamped-down vegetation that lead to and from the forest).

CAMP SUNSET

TIMOTHY LAKE,
OREGON

— Camp —

SETUP

Once you've found your site, quickly establish camp to get the hard work out of the way before going exploring. Check to see if you have dependable cell phone coverage and, if not, whether the campground has a phone for placing a 911 call, if needed.

PITCH YOUR TENT ON LEVEL GROUND

Anybody who has ever spent a restless night slowly sliding headfirst out of a sleeping bag or rolling from one side of the tent to the other knows why this is important.

SEPARATE EATING AND SLEEPING AREAS

Picnic tables and campfire circles inevitably morph into party central. Even in a small campsite, create psychological space by setting tents a few yards away.

ACCESSORIZE

Car camping lets you bring more gear than if you're backpacking in. Camp chairs and hammocks make a convivial campsite; lanterns make it cheery at night.

— Before You Unpack —

It might seem obsessive to clean up before you start putting up a tent. But the practice helps maintain a clean campsite for the rest of the trip. And that's especially important in ecologically sensitive campsites, where microtrash and even small bits of food can hurt an animal's diet.

Pitch a Tent

*Tent designs vary by model, but some universal principles apply.
If you have a new tent or a newly borrowed one, it's a good idea to practice
setting up in the backyard before your trip. That's the perfect time to
double-check you have all the tent parts too.*

1. PREP THE SPACE AND UNPACK

Find the flattest, most debris-free area of the campsite. Clear the tent setup area of any branches, loose rocks, and pinecones. Unpack the tent and set out all its parts. Make sure that all zippers are closed.

2. SET OUT THE GROUND CLOTH

Spread the ground cloth or footprint (see page 29) over the flattest area of the site.

3. ROLL OUT THE TENT

Arrange your tent over the ground cloth, orienting the tent the way you'll want it to stand. Except in hot conditions, the door should face away from the prevailing winds to prevent breezes from filling your tent and potentially dislodging it. If the site has a slope, position the tent door downhill so that rain can't flow inside.

4. ASSEMBLE THE POLES

With shock-corded poles, gently pull them into position section by section to reduce long-term wear and tear.

5. ATTACH THE POLES

Begin attaching the poles to the tent, using the sleeves or clips to thread them into position, from one corner to the opposite corner. Ease the poles into place to avoid tearing the tent. Once the poles are in position through the corner rings, they should form a frame along the roofline.

6. ANCHOR IT DOWN

Using the grommets or webbing straps and a mallet, drive stakes into the ground at a 45° angle to make the tent corners taut. Add more stakes to tighten the rest of the tent. In windy conditions, you may have to add staked rope on the side of the tent facing into the breeze.

7. ATTACH THE RAIN FLY

Once the tent is standing, attach the rain fly. Make sure the front of the fly lines up with the tent door.

8. TUCK IN THE EDGES

Check to see that the ground cloth doesn't extend beyond the tent. Tuck its edges under the tent to keep it from collecting any rain.

Commandments

If your tent will be exposed to the sun for an extended time, put on the rain fly.

— Always —

take off shoes and boots before entering. Leave them close for easy access.

FOR ADDITIONAL PROTECTION AND COMFORT, USE A SLEEPING BAG LINER.

WEAR CLEAN CLOTHES TO BED.

Set aside some items that you use only for sleeping and stash them in a protected spot during the day. You'll stay much more comfortable, and your sleeping bag will last longer.

NEVER EAT
— or —
KEEP FOOD

in the tent. Food can attract animals, from ants and mice to grizzly bears. Consider yourself warned.

KEEP ALL

flames, including lighters and old-fashioned fuel-burning lanterns, **OUT** of the tent.

Tie a Knot

While there are hundreds of knots you could put to use in the outdoors, these three are a great place to start. Free end or free line refers to the working section of the rope, while the standing end or line is the section that you're not actively using.

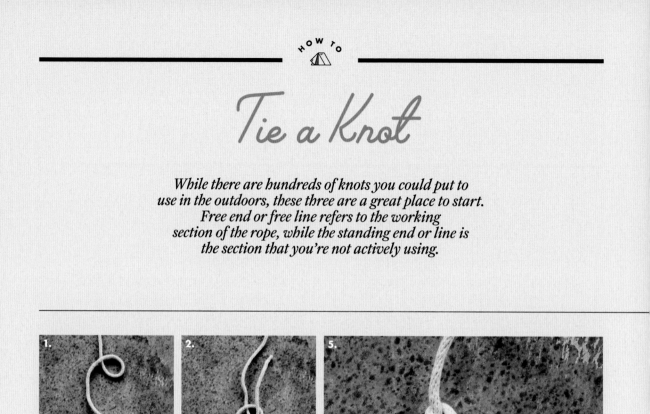

BOWLINE

Strong and secure, bowline (pronounced *bo-lin*) knots form fixed loops at the end of a rope and have many uses, including hanging hammocks and securing canoes and kayaks.

1. Create a small loop in a line, looping toward yourself, and allow the free end of the rope to hang down.

2. Take the free end and bring it through the loop from underneath.

3. Direct it above the loop near the standing line, creating a second small loop, then pass the free end under and around the standing line.

4. Lead the free end through the upper loop (the loop closest to the standing line), letting the free end dangle.

5. Cinch the knot to tighten.

CLOVE HITCH

An all-purpose, easy-to-tie knot for attaching lines to objects, the clove hitch is also easy to untie, though not as secure as some other options.

1. Bring the free end around a post or tree. Cross the free end over the standing line on the front of the pole.

2. Wrap the line a second time around the post below the first coil you created, then tuck the free end under this last wrap.

3. Tighten the knot.

  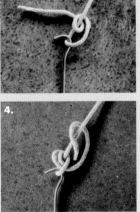

TAUT-LINE HITCH

This is a good knot for tightening guy lines around tent stakes and for setting up tarps.

1. Bring the free end of the rope around an anchor such as a stake or a tree, then pull the free end through the loop you've created.

2. Wrap the free end around the standing line once again, wrapping toward the anchor as you create the coils.

3. Pull the free end through the loop again.

4. Bring the free line around and under the standing line, but this time, outside the coils you've created (on the side farther from the stake), pulling the line through this new loop to create a third coil.

5. Cinch the knot tight and you should be able to freely move the knot to tighten the rope around the anchor.

— Setting up —
THE KITCHEN

*An organized kitchen area is as much a necessity outdoors as it is at home.
Take your cues from these tips and you'll soon be ready to feed an army of hungry campers.*

ESTABLISH YOUR KITCHEN AREA adjacent to a picnic table, if one is available. Not all sites have tables, so check in advance and bring along a lightweight (but sturdy) folding table if needed. If possible, make sure that the kitchen is at a good distance (at least 30 feet) from any tents, brush, and vegetation.

PLACE COOLERS IN A SHADED AREA to extend the life of your ice and to better keep food cold.

TRY TO SET UP THE KITCHEN downwind from tents and at a distance to avoid having cooking odors fill your sleeping space.

CREATE A "NO-FLY ZONE" AROUND the kitchen. That means the kids shouldn't run or play anywhere in the cooking area and that the space is free of tripping hazards.

SEPARATE COOKING AND PREP. Put your stove, fuel, and oven mitts at one end of the table. Cover the rest of the table with a waterproof cloth. Use that area for food prep, then clear it away as needed for meals. After you eat, put the table to work for washing and drying dishes (you can spread them out to air dry). If you don't have adequate surfaces, improvise by putting down a waterproof cloth in the storage area of an SUV and using that space for some prep.

STASH POTS AND PANS UNDERNEATH the table in a container, or on top of your campsite's bear box, if it has one.

DEDICATE ONE LANTERN SPECIFICALLY to the kitchen area.

SET UP A SEPARATE CLEANING AREA on a second table if available. (See "Washing Dishes in Camp," page 83.)

KEEP TRASH AND RECYCLING BAGS accessible by hanging them from a tree that's convenient to the kitchen. Remember to empty them in the campground bins after meals, or stash them in a bear locker so they don't attract critters.

PITCH A TARP above the kitchen if you're camping in a rainy area or a site exposed to the sun.

Build a Campfire

First, early humans discovered fire. Then they learned how to tame it and build campfires. And not long after that, they invented marshmallows for s'mores. The campfire is the heart and soul of your site: the place where everyone gathers, whether for warmth, cooking, or storytelling.

GATHERING FIRE MATERIALS

- Always check whether the campground has regulations about collecting wood for fires or bringing wood from home. Ideally, you want a mix of sizes; see step 1 at right.
- Never chop or break branches from either living or dead standing trees.
- The wood you use should be dry. If it doesn't break with a sharp cracking sound, the wood is too wet and will produce a lot of smoke while not burning well.
- Don't collect rotting wood. It doesn't burn well and is an important source of soil nutrients.
- Bring or gather more fire materials than you think you'll need. You don't want to start scrambling for wood in the dark if the fire starts dying down sooner than expected.

1. CHOOSE THE RIGHT SPOT AND SET OUT FUEL

Use existing firepits if available. When this isn't an option, find a clear spot that is at least 15 feet from tents, shrubs, and other flammable objects. Remove any branches, leaves, and ground debris. Dig a shallow pit and enclose it with rocks.

Set out a mix of tinder, kindling, and logs. You'll also need newspaper and either matches or a lighter.

2. BUILD

Our favorite design combines a log cabin–style arrangement on the outside with a tipi of smaller wood in the middle touching the logs to help them catch. In a fire ring, place four large logs in a box shape (use six if you need to plan for a long cooking time). Add tinder inside the box.

3. ADD KINDLING AND LIGHT TINDER

Arrange kindling in a tipi over tinder. Light tinder in several places. When the pile starts smoking, blow on it gently until flames emerge.

4. LET IT BURN

It takes about 1 to 1½ hours for a campfire to burn down to low flames plus embers, the ideal stage for cooking. This is your golden time for happy hour and dinner prep. For more specific tips on cooking over a campfire, see page 81.

5. PUT IT OUT RIGHT

Stop adding fuel at least an hour before you plan to leave camp or go to bed. Once wood has been reduced to coal and ash, spread out the remains and douse with plenty of water or dirt. Stir everything in the pit with a shovel or tongs. Leave your campsite only when the campfire is completely extinguished.

— Campground —
ETIQUETTE

Meet "That Guy." Or perhaps you already know him (or her).
He's the one wearing the T-shirt that reads, "Freedom's Just Another Word
for Me Getting to Do Whatever I Want, Whenever I Want to Do It."
No sir, don't tread on him. The truth is that there's a little of That Guy in all of us,
so here are a few reminders for basic camping etiquette. Just in case.

HONOR YOUR BORDERS. Never cut through other camp-sites, and keep a watch on the kids and dogs too. Even if the adjacent campsite is empty, that doesn't give you the right to spread out into it.

SET UP BEFORE DARK. It's much harder to establish camp at night, and you'll end up keeping other campers awake. Hence all that stinkeye directed your way come morning.

KEEP THE CAR DOORS OPEN WHILE UNPACKING. Slamming doors are unnecessary. Get everything out before gently closing the doors.

RESPECT SHARED SPACES. The bathroom sink is no place to scrub out burnt stew from your dutch oven. Limit your shower time, both to save water and to give others their chance.

DON'T OVERPOPULATE YOUR CAMPSITE. If you have a large group, spread out over a few campsites or check into the availability of a group campground instead of clogging one site. That reunion of 20 of your besties may be fun for you but totally overwhelming for everyone else.

RESPECT PERSONAL SPACE. If you're in a relatively uncrowded first-come, first-served campground, set up at a distance from other campers. Ever have someone stand too close to you in an empty elevator?

OBEY QUIET TIME. This ain't no party, this ain't no disco: Most campers are up with the sun. And remember that there's no such thing as a soundproof tent.

KEEP IT ON THE DOWN LOW. Direct headlamps and flash-lights toward the ground to prevent beams from blinding your campmates and shining into tents.

UNPLUG. A bit of campfire "Kumbaya" is one thing. But whether your tastes run to EDM or AC/DC, your amplified personal soundtrack can be an intrusion to fellow campers, most of whom are seeking peace and quiet in nature. Cell phones, tablets, DVD players, and loud generators can also break the spell of camping.

NO FIREWORKS. That includes on the Fourth of July. Fireworks disturb the peace, as well as wildlife, and pose a fire threat.

SERENITY NOW: BE TOLERANT. Expect to sacrifice some privacy and to deal with other people's foibles. The good news is that the vast majority of campers are also considerate and hoping for a tranquil escape from their daily routines.

— *Beware* —
CAMPGROUND NEMESES

Bears are often on people's minds, but you're more likely to battle mice, squirrels, and raccoons. Ask rangers or camp hosts about any recent animal activity, and remember just a few precautions that can keep you safe and your tent free of unwanted animals.

1. Do not think you are faster or smarter than a raccoon or bear. See our tips on dealing with bears in the wild (pages 164 and 165).
2. Never leave food out in your campsite, then walk away "for just a minute," thinking that raccoons or pesky bluejays won't get it. See #1 above.
3. Never bring food into your tent. Remove food from your day pack and put it in a bear box (see below) or lock food in your car with the windows rolled up.
4. Bear-resistant food boxes and canisters are also raccoon-resistant. These are your friends. Use them. Store canisters 100 feet from sleeping areas.
5. Keep it clean. Wash your pots, pans, and dishes, and clean food residue out of firepits to avoid leaving anything out for critters who are out looking for a midnight snack.
6. Avoid the use of perfumed or aromatic personal products—deodorants, hair products, and lotions—that could draw bears and other wildlife.

HOW TO AVOID COMMON PROBLEMS

In addition to the usual cuts, scrapes, and blisters, here's an assortment of common camping hazards to be prepared for. Carry a first-aid kit and a manual for reference so you can treat various ailments, but the key is to prevent problems before they happen.

BEES, WASPS, YELLOW JACKETS, AND HORNETS

Expect a variety of unwanted guests at your campsite, including this Un-Fab Four. Sweets and meats will lure bees and yellow jackets, so keep foods stored in sealed containers as much as possible during prep and meals. (Some people also set out a small piece of meat away from the table as a decoy when these guys start getting interested.) Scented items and even bright clothing can also draw these stinging insects. If you notice hives or swarming clusters near your campsite, move to another location.

WASP

HONEYBEE

TICKS

There's nothing quite like feeling an irritating bite, then looking down to see a tick as it attaches itself. Worse yet, they can carry illnesses, including Lyme disease. Wearing long sleeves and pants, tucking shirts in, and pulling socks over your pants cuffs will limit entry points. Light-colored clothing makes it easier to spot ticks. Remove them by using fine-tipped tweezers to grasp the tick as closely to the skin surface as you can. Slowly and carefully pull straight out to avoid breaking the tick off and leaving its head inside the skin (if part of the tick is still embedded, try to remove it as you would a splinter). Throw the tick into rubbing alcohol to kill it, and clean the bite area with alcohol or an antibacterial agent. Keep watch on the bite victim for fevers, headaches, and rashes.

SNAKES

The good news is that snakes really don't want to have anything to do with you. Keep the tent zipped to prevent snakes from crawling inside to explore, and shake out sleeping bags. Use care when collecting wood, and don't reach into gaps between boulders or logs if you can't see what's inside. On cool mornings, rattlesnakes like to warm up on sunny patches along trails and fire roads, so be sure to look ahead of where you're walking.

POISON OAK, IVY, AND SUMAC

Familiarize the whole family with these plants, which can cause itchy rashes and blistered skin after contact, and look for any stands in immediate proximity to the campsite. Poison oak, which is found in the West, is recognizable by its clusters of three leaves; poison ivy (also with three-leaf clusters) and poison sumac (7- to 13-leaf clusters) grow in the East and Midwest. Clothes and shoes that have brushed up against these plants need a thorough cleaning with soap and water or a commercial preparation such as Tecnu to prevent ongoing exposure.

STINGING NETTLES

Stinging nettles grow as bushy colonies in moist areas, such as along creeks, and are common in areas with high rainfall, including the Northwest. Hairs on the leaf and stem surfaces act like miniature needles that inject skin with substances that lead to itching and burning.

MINOR BURNS

With less space than your stove back home, camp stoves quickly heat up the handles on pots and pans, so always use an oven mitt or gripper. Take care around campfires, especially when the kids are cooking marshmallows for s'mores and may inadvertently grab a hot cooking fork.

ALTITUDE SICKNESS

Some people arriving from lower elevations have trouble acclimating to the reduced oxygen availability of high-altitude areas and may experience shortness of breath and/or dizziness. Take it slowly at first if you've driven from sea level into the mountains above 8,000 feet. Proper diet and hydration can limit symptoms, which may include nausea and headaches.

POISON IVY

HEAT-RELATED ILLNESSES

Cramping, heat exhaustion, and heatstroke can all occur without adequate hydration and places to escape from the sun, especially during and after hikes and other exercise. Drink fluids with electrolytes to maintain salt levels in the blood, and take note of such indicators as dizziness, disorientation, and rapid heartbeat.

HYPOTHERMIA

Although most people associate hypothermia with frigid winter temperatures, this uncontrolled loss of body temperature can also occur during swims in cold water or while wearing wet clothes in windy and cool conditions. If you notice shivering, a lack of coordination, or slurring speech, get warm and dry as quickly—and gently—as possible, using blankets, non-alcoholic beverages, or body heat.

LEAVE
— No —
TRACE

Camping is a low-impact, rather than no-impact, way to travel, one of those Zen riddles in which we're all part of the problem and all part of the solution too. Adhere to the following guidelines from the Leave No Trace Center for Outdoor Ethics, an organization based in Boulder, Colorado, and you can minimize impacts both on the environment and on your fellow campers.

Plan ahead and prepare

Reduce waste before you leave home by repacking food and getting rid of wrappings and other packaging. Check in advance about any regulations, such as restrictions on collecting wood and lighting campfires.

Travel and camp on durable surfaces

Try to use existing fire rings and campsites when in an area without formal facilities, especially wilderness areas. Keep to official trails or walk on rocks, gravel, and dried grasses instead of living vegetation.

Dispose of waste properly

Pack it in, pack it out is the guiding principle. Before you leave the campsite, pick up any trash or food, and leave the area cleaner than you found it. To further appease the camping gods, dispose of other garbage too, even if it's not yours.

Stay clear of water sources

Set up camp 200 feet (about 70 paces) or more from lakes and streams to lessen the effect on water quality and the chance of disrupting wildlife that comes down to drink. When cleaning dishes (or yourself) use only biodegradable soaps in small quantities. Hand sanitizers reduce water usage and the potential impact of soapy water that gets poured out. And when dumping dishwater, spread it around instead of pouring it all out at one spot.

Leave what you find

If you come upon a fossil, arrowhead, or beautiful rock, it's easy to think, Well, what's the harm in just taking one? But many are protected, especially in state and national parks, so leave them where they are. If nothing else, be superstitious: In Hawaii, you hear endless stories about people sending back chunks of lava to the islands after encountering bad luck when they took the rocks home.

Minimize campfire impact

Everyone loves a roaring campfire—which can be an issue if it gets too big. Use a lightweight stove for most of your cooking, and keep campfires small, in established fire rings. And be sure to completely extinguish fires. Some people also clean out the remaining ashes. For more on campfires, see page 66.

Respect wildlife

You're on their turf, so don't be rude. Keep a distance while observing animals, especially when they're with young or nesting. Never feed wildlife, because animals that associate humans with food can become nuisances or even dangerous. Store your food so it doesn't present a temptation. And don't let dogs disturb the local inhabitants.

Be considerate of other visitors

The Golden Rule applies equally to camping. Make sure you keep campground etiquette (see page 69) in mind.

— *Breaking* —

CAMP

You've had the time of your life, but when it's time to go, here are a few things to remember.

PREP YOUR SLEEPING GEAR: Before putting your sleeping bag into a stuff sack, hang it up to dry any moisture from the previous night while you take care of other tasks. Deflate inflatable sleeping pads or air mattresses. This will go faster if you undo the valve while still lying down.

PUT ASIDE ITEMS YOU NEED during the day, including food and maps, and fill water bottles for the trip home.

CLEAN ANY DIRT off stakes and poles, as well as the bottom of the tent and the ground cloth.

IF YOU CAN, GIVE THE TENT and rain fly a chance to dry before packing them. Otherwise, dry them out at home so they don't mildew.

WIPE THE STOVE and kitchen items before packing.

CHECK THE FIRE RING to make sure that there's no lingering hot ash.

ONCE YOU'VE LOADED UP the car, have everyone stroll slowly back through the campsite to check for overlooked gear and trash you may have missed.

75

WONDER LAKE CAMPGROUND,
DENALI NATIONAL PARK, ALASKA

CHAPTER 3

THE BEST
CAMP FOOD
Ever

Hunger. Fire. Food. There's nothing like camp cooking to bring life's most basic elements into sharp focus and a happy resolution. GETTING DELICIOUS FOOD ON THE TABLE offers much more too. Preparing even the simplest recipe, be it for pancakes or margaritas, connects you with your fellow campers—and with nature—each time you create a meal together under the open sky.

— Cooking on a —
CAMP STOVE

Using a standard two-burner camp stove is not that different from using your home stove. Basically, just turn the camp stove on and start cooking (see page 40). For camping newbies, though, mastering a few details makes the difference between ease and frustration.

CONNECT STOVE TO FUEL

The most common camp stoves come with either a separate pipe or a hose that's attached for connecting the stove to the fuel (usually, propane canisters). First, attach the valve on the connector to the opening on the fuel canister by pressing down while turning until you meet resistance. For a connector pipe, attach the other end to the stove: Push it into the opening on the side of the stove and turn the nut on the pipe until tight. Finally, arrange the canister on its side to the back or side of the stove so the fuel will flow easily.

CHECK THAT THE STOVE IS LEVEL

If water in a skillet on the stove all flows to one side, your picnic table isn't level—and in most places,

you can't move it. Some stoves have self-leveling feet. You can also buy separate leg levelers. Also try shifting the stove to another part of the table, or seating a small, flat rock under one of the stove's edges.

DON'T FORGET THE WINDSCREENS

Most stoves come with windscreens attached; set them in place, and you'll get the stove lit and the food cooked a lot faster. The Coleman model shown above features burners with built-in windscreens.

GO FOR NEW-SCHOOL IGNITION

Turn the knob to start the fuel flowing, and light the flame (butane lighters work even in wind and drizzle). Some stoves offer click-on ignition too.

— Using a —
CAMP GRILL

Most campsites come with a metal fire ring that has a built-in cooking grate for use over a wood fire, or a box-shaped grill for use with charcoal. While a wood fire offers more romance, charcoal is faster, and both types work well for cooking. In either case, cooking grates sometimes need a wipe-down with paper towels and a little vegetable oil to get rid of rust. Also, the grilling surface is likely smaller than you're used to at home, so for large groups you'll be cooking food in batches.

HOW TO BUILD A CHARCOAL FIRE

Fill a chimney starter with charcoal briquets and crumple newspaper into the base. Set chimney on a camp charcoal grill, ignite the paper, and let charcoal burn until it ignites, 15 to 20 minutes. Wearing grilling gloves, dump charcoal onto base of grill and spread with tongs. Set the cooking grate in place. If needed, let the fire burn to the heat specified in a recipe, measured by how long you can hold a hand above the grate. For dutch oven cooking, see page 112.

HOW TO BUILD A CAMPFIRE FOR COOKING

For those who didn't grow up as cave people—or Boy or Girl Scouts—cooking over a campfire may not come naturally. Start with the combo design explained on page 66, then fine-tune your skills with the following tips.

Use enough fuel

Four logs works for a quick grill, but start with six if you're cooking over an extended period. Keep an extra log burning at the back of the fire ring.

Plan ahead

Remember it takes 1 to 1$^1/_2$ hours for a fire to burn to low flames plus embers, the ideal stage for cooking.

Adjust the fire

Spread the fire under the cooking grate, using grilling tongs. As you cook, move logs or add fuel as needed.

WASHING DISHES
— in Camp —

After you've cleared up from a meal, turn your picnic table or one of its benches into a dishwashing station. Or use a second table, if you have one.

SCRAPE FOOD FROM PLATES

A little advance work with a scraper or paper towel goes a long way to keeping dishwater clean.

ORGANIZE A BUCKET SYSTEM

Two bins, nesting basins, or collapsible sinks are optimal: one for hot soapy water (heat it on the stove, and add only a small amount of biodegradable soap), and the second for rinsing (ideally with hot water). If you don't have bins or sinks, improvise by washing and then rinsing in a pasta pot. If you're camping in an area without potable water, add a third basin for a sanitizing cold-water rinse with a capful of bleach. Fill bins only about halfway to avoid wasting water.

SET OUT DISHES TO DRY

Once dishes are clean, arrange them upside down on your picnic table to dry (preferably on a waterproof tablecloth), tipping them onto each other a bit to let air circulate.

DISPOSE OF WATER

Pour all the dishwater into one bucket. Strain food scraps from the water (they attract animals and are unsightly if dumped out), and take them to the trash. Broadcast dishwater in your campsite, or in another area if directed to by the campground.

CARING FOR CAST IRON

Given a little TLC, the same cast-iron skillet and dutch oven—which stand up to camp stoves and campfires and cook your food evenly—will serve your grandchildren just as well.

MAINTAIN THE PATINA. Over time, cast-iron cookware develops a beautiful seasoned surface that's naturally nonstick. A lot of new cast ironware gives you a jump-start on this process, as it's sold preseasoned (baked at a high temperature with a coating of oil), so all you have to do is maintain it.

WASH AND DRY IT RIGHT. After you use a pan, hand-wash it each time with hot water—no soap—and a sponge or plastic mesh scrubber. Heat the pan on a camp stove or over the fire to drive off any moisture. Then rub the warm pan with a paper towel and enough vegetable oil to coat lightly. This maintains the seasoning and keeps moisture out so the pan won't rust.

GET THE
— *Kids* —
TO HELP

There are a few secrets to getting kids to help with camp cooking, and also to getting them excited about what they're eating. At home, talk about what they might enjoy and look through recipes, so they can nominate a few favorites. In camp, match kitchen tasks to the children's ages and skill levels.

Younger kids can snip herbs with children's scissors, slice softer foods (cucumbers, bananas) with serrated plastic knives, and swish and tear lettuce. Older kids can peel vegetables and use paring knives (with adult supervision) to cut carrots and small potatoes. And everybody can help wash the dishes.

For recipes especially designed for kids, try Hands-on Salad (page 137), Italian-Style Hobo Bundles (page 125), and One-Pan Mac 'n' Cheese (page 129).

HIGH
– *Altitude* –
BAKING TIPS

On any given mountain, you're likely to find a frustrated baker. That's because most baking recipes, including ours for camp, are developed and tested for use from sea level to about 3,000 feet. With the help of high-altitude baking authorities Pat Kendall, formerly of the Colorado State University Cooperative Extension, and Nancy Feldman, formerly at the University of California Cooperative Extension, and also by consulting the invaluable book *Pie in the Sky* by Susan G. Purdy (William Morrow, 2005), we've assembled some guidelines that should allow you to bake successfully above 3,000 feet.

At high altitudes, liquid boils at lower temperatures (below 212°) and moisture evaporates more quickly—both of which significantly impact the quality of baked goods. Leavening gases (air, carbon dioxide, water vapor) expand faster. Also, flour tends to absorb more liquid in the low humidity of high altitudes. If you're camping at 3,000 feet or below, first try a recipe as is. Sometimes few, if any, changes are needed. But the higher you go, the more you'll have to adjust your recipe.

For quick breads such as biscuits, cornbread, cakes, and pancakes, try decreasing baking powder or soda by 1/8 or 1/4 teaspoon per teaspoon called for. If that's not working, cut back on flour by about 2 tablespoons per cup called for.

For yeast breads, you may need less flour, so mix in about two-thirds of what's called for in the recipe, then check the dough to see whether it looks and feels the way it does at sea level before adding more. Keep an eye on the dough's rise; yeast doughs rise more quickly—sometimes twice as fast—in the reduced pressure of higher altitudes. Instead of letting dough rise until doubled in volume, let it rise only about a third. That will compensate for its tendency to over-expand as it bakes in the dutch oven.

GUIDE TO NUTRITIONAL INFORMATION FOR RECIPES

GF (GLUTEN-FREE)
No wheat, rye, barley, or oats. Check any processed food ingredients you use to verify they're gluten-free.

LC (LOW-CALORIE)
Less than 500 calories for a main dish, 250 for a side dish, 150 for an appetizer, and 350 for dessert.

LS (LOW-SODIUM)
Less than 500 mg for a main dish, and 350 for a side dish, appetizer, or dessert.

V (VEGETARIAN)
Contains no meat products.

VG (VEGAN)
Contains no animal products, including gelatin made with animal-derived ingredients.

HEARTY WHOLE-GRAIN PANCAKES with BLUEBERRIES

Makes mix for 4 batches (each 8 to 10 pancakes)
15 minutes at home; 15 minutes in camp

Take a few minutes at home to whip up your own pancake mix, and you'll have homemade pancakes in camp that are just as fast as instant and a whole lot tastier.

PANCAKE MIX

2½ cups all-purpose flour
  3 cups whole-wheat flour
  ¼ cup each wheat bran and wheat germ
  ¼ cup packed light brown sugar
  1 tablespoon *each* baking powder and kosher salt
1½ teaspoons baking soda
1½ cups buttermilk powder*

PANCAKES WITH BLUEBERRIES (1 BATCH)

  2 cups pancake mix (above)
  2 large eggs
    About 4 tablespoons vegetable oil, divided
  1 cup blueberries
    Butter and maple syrup

AT HOME

1. Make pancake mix: Whisk together ingredients in a large bowl and transfer to a container with a lid or a resealable plastic bag.

IN CAMP

2. Make pancakes: Whisk together 2 cups mix with 1¼ cups water, the eggs, and 2 tablespoons oil in a large bowl until mostly smooth. Heat a large cast-iron skillet over medium heat on a camp stove and grease skillet with ½ tablespoon oil. Ladle ⅓-cup portions of batter into skillet. Cook, turning once, until pancakes are golden brown and cooked through, about 5 minutes. Add 1 teaspoon oil to skillet and repeat with more batter to cook remaining pancakes. Serve with blueberries, butter, and syrup.

*Find buttermilk powder at well-stocked grocery stores.

MAKE AHEAD *The mix, up to 2 weeks, stored airtight.*

PER 2-PANCAKE SERVING 390 Cal., 41% (160 Cal.) from fat; 13 g protein; 18 g fat (3.1 g sat.); 42 g carbo (4.5 g fiber); 307 mg sodium; 101 mg chol. **LC/LS/V**

MASCARPONE FRENCH TOAST with WARM BLACKBERRY SYRUP

Serves 4 | 35 minutes in camp

For guests of Sealegs Kayaking Adventures of Vancouver Island, B.C., the morning often starts with this decadent twist on French toast.

  1 large egg
  ½ cup milk
  ¼ cup sugar
  2 teaspoons cinnamon
1½ teaspoons vanilla extract, divided
1½ cups cold mascarpone cheese
  2 tablespoons blackberry liqueur
  8 thick (¾ inch) slices day-old wide French bread, such as bâtard
  ¼ cup maple syrup
2½ cups blackberries
  2 tablespoons salted butter
    Cooked bacon

1. Whisk together egg, milk, sugar, cinnamon, and ½ teaspoon vanilla in a large bowl.

2. In another bowl, stir together mascarpone, remaining 1 teaspoon vanilla, and the liqueur. Spread mascarpone mixture over 4 bread slices; top with remaining slices.

3. Cook maple syrup and berries in a small covered saucepan over medium-high heat on a camp stove until berries start to break down, 5 to 10 minutes. Remove from heat.

4. Heat a large heavy frying pan or 2 smaller ones over medium-high heat; swirl butter in pan(s). Dip sandwiches in egg mixture, then cook, turning once, until crisp and browned, 4 to 8 minutes total. Serve French toast with syrup and bacon.

PER SERVING (WITHOUT BACON) 1,215 Cal., 65% (792 Cal.) from fat; 26 g protein; 88 g fat (47 g sat.); 86 g carbo (7.5 g fiber); 705 mg sodium; 281 mg chol. **V (WITHOUT BACON)**

MASCARPONE
FRENCH TOAST

BREAKFAST SHAKSHOUKA

Serves 6 | 1 hour in camp

To scoop up every bit of this spicy egg and tomato dish, popular in North Africa and Israel, you owe yourself some grilled toast. Brush slices of rustic bread with olive oil, then toast them on a grill pan set on a camp stove.

> About ¼ cup extra-virgin olive oil, divided
> 1 small onion, chopped
> ¾ cup chopped fresh Anaheim chiles or 1 can (4 ounces) chopped Anaheim chiles, drained
> 2 garlic cloves, chopped
> 1 teaspoon ground cumin
> About ½ teaspoon kosher salt
> 1 tablespoon sweet or hot paprika
> 1 can (28 ounces) crushed tomatoes
> 2 teaspoons sugar
> ¼ cup chopped flat-leaf parsley, divided
> 6 large eggs
> Pepper
> ½ cup crumbled feta cheese

1. Heat 2 tablespoons oil in a 12-inch cast-iron skillet over medium-high heat on a camp stove. Sauté onion and fresh chiles, if using, until softened, 7 to 8 minutes. Add canned chiles, if using, garlic, cumin, ½ teaspoon salt, and the paprika; cook, stirring, until garlic is softened, about 1 minute.

2. Add tomatoes and sugar; bring to a simmer, then reduce heat and cook until flavors are blended and mixture is a little thicker, about 15 minutes. Stir in 1 tablespoon parsley.

3. With a wooden spoon, make 6 depressions in the tomato mixture. Crack 1 egg into each and sprinkle with salt and pepper. Cover skillet tightly with a lid or foil. Cook until eggs are set but yolks are still runny, rotating skillet 180° halfway through cooking, 5 to 9 minutes.

4. Scatter feta and remaining 3 tablespoons parsley over shakshouka, then drizzle with remaining 2 tablespoons oil. Serve with more oil at the table if you like.

PER SERVING 249 Cal., 62% (154 Cal.) from fat; 12 g protein; 18 g fat (4.8 g sat.); 15 g carbo (3.3 g fiber); 584 mg sodium; 223 mg chol. **GF/LC/V**

HUEVOS RANCHEROS con BACON

Serves 4 | 30 minutes in camp

Gilbert Flores, a Sunset *reader from Visalia, California, shared this recipe. The sauce is easy to make, and in summer, you could double the fresh tomato and skip the canned sauce. No matter what time of year you make it, don't skip the bacon.*

> 8 ounces thick-cut bacon
> ½ white onion, chopped
> ½ green bell pepper, cut into ½-inch dice
> 1 jalapeño chile, halved and thinly sliced
> 1 medium tomato, chopped
> 1 can (8 ounces) tomato sauce
> 8 large eggs
> Warm corn tortillas* and refried beans

1. Set a large frying pan over medium-high heat on a camp stove. Cook bacon, turning often, until almost crisp, about 10 minutes. Transfer to paper towels.

2. Drain most of fat from pan and reserve. Add onion, pepper, and chile to pan and cook until starting to soften, about 2 minutes. Stir in tomato, tomato sauce, and ½ cup water. Bring to a simmer.

3. Meanwhile, working in batches, heat a little reserved fat and fry the eggs in a large seasoned cast-iron skillet or nonstick frying pan (discard the rest of fat*). Set tortillas on each plate and top with 2 eggs. Spoon sauce over eggs and crumble bacon on top. Serve with refried beans.

*To warm tortillas, wrap in foil and heat directly over camp stove, turning often. Mop up leftover bacon fat with paper towels and discard with garbage so it doesn't attract animals in camp.

PER SERVING 256 Cal., 57% (146 Cal.) from fat; 20 g protein; 16 g fat (5.3 g sat.); 7.4 g carbo (1.8 g fiber); 826 mg sodium; 390 mg chol. **GF/LC**

SKILLET BREAKFAST POTATOES

Makes 5 cups; serves 4 | 35 minutes in camp

Starting with raw potato slices rather than boiled makes them come out nice and crusty. Add a fried egg or two, and you can call it a meal. You'll need a vegetable peeler and a wide metal spatula.

1½ pounds thin-skinned potatoes, such as Yukon Gold
¼ cup olive oil
1½ teaspoons kosher salt, divided
½ each red and yellow bell pepper, cut into chunks (or use one kind)
½ onion, coarsely chopped
½ teaspoon pepper
3 handfuls (3 cups) baby spinach leaves

1. Peel potatoes, cut in half lengthwise, and slice crosswise ¼ inch thick. Heat oil in a large cast-iron skillet over medium-high heat on a camp stove. Stir in potatoes and 1 teaspoon salt. Cook, stirring occasionally, until potatoes begin to turn golden, 5 to 10 minutes.

2. Add bell peppers, onion, remaining ½ teaspoon salt, and the pepper. Cook, turning occasionally with a wide metal spatula, until potatoes are tender and well browned, about 15 minutes; reduce heat if they start to brown too quickly. Stir in spinach and cook until wilted, about 2 minutes.

PER SERVING 258 Cal., 47% (120 Cal.) from fat; 3.3 g protein; 14 g fat (1.9 g sat.); 33 g carbo (6.2 g fiber); 601 mg sodium; 0 mg chol. **GF/VG**

PIZZA SCRAMBLED EGGS

Serves 4 to 6 | 15 minutes in camp

Who doesn't love "pizza-flavored," especially applied to breakfast? In this case, we're talking sausage, pepperoni, olives, and tomatoes. But feel free to customize the add-ins to suit your campers, using either one big cast-iron skillet or up to four small (6½-inch) ones (with this size, cook roughly one-quarter of the recipe at a time).

1 mild or hot Italian sausage
9 large eggs
1 teaspoon dried basil
½ teaspoon each kosher salt and pepper
2 tablespoons olive oil
20 thin slices pepperoni (about 2 ounces), cut into ½-inch-wide strips
1 cup shredded mozzarella cheese
6 tablespoons grated parmesan cheese
1 can (2¼ ounces) sliced ripe black olives, drained
½ cup cherry tomatoes, cut in half
4 green onions, thinly sliced

1. Squeeze sausage from casing into a large cast-iron skillet and cook over medium-high heat on a camp stove until browned, breaking meat into small chunks, 4 to 5 minutes.

2. Meanwhile, in a large bowl, whisk eggs, basil, salt, and pepper to blend well.

3. Reduce heat to medium. Add oil and pepperoni to skillet and cook, stirring, until pepperoni is very lightly browned, about 30 seconds. Pour in eggs and cook, stirring occasionally, until they're halfway set, 1 to 2 minutes. Reduce heat to low and stir in remaining ingredients. Cook, stirring gently a couple more times, until cheeses melt and eggs are set, 2 to 3 minutes more.

PER SERVING 316 Cal., 69% (218 Cal.) from fat; 23 g protein; 24 g fat (8.2 g sat.); 3.8 g carbo (1.0 g fiber); 780 mg sodium; 356 mg chol. **GF**

PIZZA SCRAMBLED
EGGS

SESAME, ALMOND,
and CHERRY GRANOLA

SESAME, ALMOND, and CHERRY GRANOLA

Makes 8 cups | 40 minutes at home

One strategy for easy breakfasts in camp: Make a batch of this deeply toasted, crunchy granola at home, and just spoon it into bowls when you wake up in the woods. (It's also excellent with fresh fruit on top, and makes an amazing snack too.) We adapted a recipe from Whole-Grain Mornings *(Ten Speed Press, 2013) by Megan Gordon, creator of artisan Marge Granola in Seattle.*

    3 cups regular (not quick-cooking or instant) rolled oats
    ¾ cup each raw sesame seeds and sliced almonds
    1 teaspoon each kosher salt and cinnamon
    ¼ teaspoon cardamom
    ½ cup each extra-virgin olive oil and honey
    1 teaspoon vanilla
    1 cup chopped dried tart cherries

1. Preheat oven to 350° and line a rimmed baking sheet with parchment paper.

2. In a large bowl, combine oats, sesame seeds, almonds, salt, and spices. In a small bowl, whisk together oil, honey, and vanilla. Add oil mixture to oat mixture and stir to combine well. Spread mixture evenly in lined baking sheet.

3. Bake granola, stirring every 10 minutes, until light brown and fragrant, 30 to 35 minutes total. Let cool in the baking sheet, then stir in cherries. Transfer to a container with a lid or a resealable plastic bag.

MAKE AHEAD *Up to 3 weeks, stored airtight.*

PER ½-CUP SERVING 239 Cal., 49% (117 Cal.) from fat; 4.5 g protein; 13 g fat (1.3 g sat.); 27 g carbo (4.9 g fiber); 108 mg sodium; 0 mg chol. LC/LS/V

OATMEAL with the WORKS

Serves 10 | 10 minutes at home; 10 minutes in camp

Add-ons, including zingy pomegranate molasses, elevate the common camp breakfast to a delectable event. If you set the items out like a topping bar, everyone can choose their favorites.

MIX
    6 cups regular or quick-cooking rolled oats
    1 cup each chopped dried apricots (preferably Blenheim) and dried tart cherries
    ½ cup packed light brown sugar
    ¾ teaspoon kosher salt (optional)

TOPPINGS
    1 cup each chocolate chips, toasted unsweetened coconut flakes, and roasted hazelnuts
    Pomegranate molasses* or brown sugar

AT HOME

1. Combine oats, apricots, cherries, and sugar, plus salt, if using, in a large bowl with hands until pieces of fruit aren't sticking together. Transfer to a container with a lid or a resealable plastic bag. Package each topping separately.

IN CAMP

2. Bring water (¾ cup per serving) to a boil in a saucepan on a camp stove and stir in oatmeal mix (¾ cup per serving). Remove from heat, cover, and let stand until most of water has been absorbed, 5 minutes. Set out with toppings.

*Find pomegranate molasses at well-stocked grocery stores.

MAKE AHEAD *The mix, up to 1 month, stored airtight.*

PER 1-CUP SERVING 501 Cal., 38% (190 Cal.) from fat; 9.7 g protein; 21 g fat (8.7 g sat.); 76 g carbo (12 g fiber); 9.2 mg sodium; 0 mg chol. LS/VG

EASY DUTCH OVEN CINNAMON ROLLS

Makes 9 | 10 minutes at home; 1½ hours in camp

The promise of eating these sweet rolls warm in camp is reason enough to pack your dutch oven. A homemade biscuit mix makes them come together in a snap.

BISCUIT MIX

4 cups flour

½ cup instant nonfat dry milk

3 tablespoons granulated sugar

2 tablespoons baking powder

1½ teaspoons table salt

¾ cup cold salted butter, cut into chunks

CINNAMON ROLLS

1 cup packed light brown sugar

2 teaspoons cinnamon

5 tablespoons salted butter, softened, divided

About 6 tablespoons flour

1¼ cups powdered sugar

AT HOME

1. Make biscuit mix: Combine dry ingredients in a large bowl. Cut in butter with a pastry blender or 2 knives until the biggest pieces are pea-size. Transfer to a lidded container or a resealable plastic bag and chill in a refrigerator or cooler until used.

2. Cut a circle of parchment paper the size of a lid of a 4-quart (10-inch) camp dutch oven. For cinnamon rolls: Combine brown sugar and cinnamon in a bowl; transfer to a lidded container or resealable plastic bag.

IN CAMP

3. Generously butter inside of dutch oven, using about 2 teaspoons butter. Set parchment circle in bottom (it will come partway up sides) and butter it. Prepare a fire (see "How to Cook in a Dutch Oven," page 112).

4. Working quickly so dough is ready to bake when coals are lit, stir biscuit mix in a large bowl with 1⅓ cups water until evenly moistened. Add an extra tablespoon water if dough seems dry. Sprinkle a large cutting board with flour and knead dough just until smooth, about 10 times.

5. Reflour board. With a floured rolling pin or wine bottle, roll out dough to a 12- by 18-inch rectangle, lifting dough and reflouring board as needed to prevent sticking. Smear remaining butter (about ¼ cup) over dough, using your fingers. (Or dot butter over dough if it's too cold to smear.) Sprinkle brown sugar mixture on top, leaving a 1½-inch strip clear along one long edge. Pat sugar firmly to help it stick.

6. Cut dough into 2- by 12-inch strips (end pieces may be a bit smaller). Roll up each strip, starting at end with sugar, and pinch seam closed. Arrange rolls cut side up in dutch oven.

7. Arrange coals for baking (see page 113). Bake cinnamon rolls 30 minutes. Evenly space 4 more lit coals on lid. Bake rolls until well browned, 10 to 20 minutes more.

8. Uncover rolls and let cool 15 minutes. In a small bowl, combine powdered sugar with 1½ tablespoons water; drizzle icing over rolls.

MAKE AHEAD *The biscuit mix, up to 1 week, chilled.*

PER ROLL 604 Cal., 33% (198 Cal.) from fat; 7.9 g protein; 22 g fat (14 g sat.); 95 g carbo (2.0 g fiber); 897 mg sodium; 58 mg chol. **V**

CHEDDAR CHEESE ROLLS

Makes 9 | 20 minutes at home; 1½ hours in camp

These incredible toasted cheese spirals start with a savory version of the biscuit mix at left.

Follow directions for Easy Dutch Oven Cinnamon Rolls, but omit granulated sugar in biscuit mix. Also omit brown sugar, cinnamon, and powdered sugar in rolls. Sprinkle buttered dough rectangle in step 5 with 2 cups **shredded sharp cheddar cheese** and pat it down.

PER ROLL 507 Cal., 53% (269 Cal.) from fat; 13 g protein; 30 g fat (19 g sat.); 46 g carbo (1.5 g fiber); 1,049 mg sodium; 80 mg chol. **V**

EASY DUTCH OVEN
CINNAMON ROLLS

CAMPGROUND CAFFÈ LATTE

Serves 4 | 15 minutes in camp

Barista-worthy coffee is as simple as getting the right ratio of grounds to water—so the joe is potent—and frothing milk with a battery-powered frother or wire whisk. We like to use a cone filter and camp coffeepot for brewing, but feel free to use a French press or another favorite method.

- 1 cup ground coffee beans, preferably dark roast, ground for a filter cone
- 2 cups whole milk

1. Line a #4 plastic coffee filter cone* with a #6 coffee filter (to avoid spilling), add coffee, and set over a camp coffeepot* or large thermos. Heat 6 cups water in a kettle or covered medium saucepan on a camp stove to just simmering (not a full boil, or coffee will get bitter). Gradually pour water over coffee.

2. In between pours, heat milk in a medium saucepan over medium-high heat, stirring often, until bubbles form at edges, about 3 minutes. Remove milk from heat and froth with a battery-powered milk frother* until you have a good layer of foam, or whisk with a wire whisk.

3. Fill mugs three-quarters full with coffee. Pour milk on top and spoon on some foam.

*Find plastic coffee filter cones at hardware and houseware stores and online. Find camp coffeepots at outdoor stores, and battery-powered frothers at kitchen stores and online.

PER SERVING 78 Cal., 46% (36 Cal.) from fat; 4.3 g protein; 4.0 g fat (2.3 g sat.); 5.9 g carbo (0 g fiber); 60 mg sodium; 12 mg chol. **GF/LC/LS/V**

CLASSIC COCOA

Makes 1 quart mix; serves 12 | 5 minutes at home; 5 minutes in camp

Few camping trips are complete without hot chocolate, and it's even better made from your own mix.

- 1 cup each granulated sugar, unsweetened cocoa powder, and powdered milk
- ½ teaspoon kosher salt
- ½ cup each miniature chocolate chips and miniature marshmallows

AT HOME

1. Combine all ingredients in a large bowl, then transfer to a container with a lid.

IN CAMP

2. For each serving, spoon ⅓ cup cocoa mix into a mug and stir in 1 cup boiling water.

MAKE AHEAD *The mix, up to 1 month, stored airtight.*

PER SERVING 142 Cal., 20% (28 Cal.) from fat; 3.7 g protein; 3.2 g fat (1.9 g sat.); 30 g carbo (2.6 g fiber); 131 mg sodium; 1 mg chol. **LC/LS/V**

MEXICAN HOT CHOCOLATE

Makes 3 cups mix; serves 9 | 10 minutes at home; 5 minutes in camp

Sweet spice and a touch of heat make this special.

- 1½ tablets Mexican chocolate, such as Ibarra or Taza
- 1 cup unsweetened cocoa powder
- 1½ cups instant nonfat dry milk
- ½ teaspoon kosher salt
- 1¼ teaspoons cinnamon
- ⅛ to ¼ teaspoon cayenne

AT HOME

1. Coarsely chop Mexican chocolate and pulse in a food processor until ground. Add remaining ingredients and whirl until smooth, then transfer to a 1-quart container.

IN CAMP

2. For each serving, spoon ⅓ cup plus 1 tablespoon cocoa mix into a mug and stir in 1 cup boiling water.

MAKE AHEAD *The mix, up to 1 month, stored airtight.*

PER ⅓-CUP SERVING 79 Cal., 22% (17 Cal.) from fat; 6.0 g protein; 1.9 g fat (1.1 g sat.); 15 g carbo (3.1 g fiber); 194 mg sodium; 1.5 mg chol. **GF/LC/LS/V**

TURKEY BLACK BEAN CHILI

Makes 3 quarts; serves 8 | 1¼ hours at home or in camp

When he was chef at Terra Bistro at Vail Mountain Lodge, Kevin Nelson (now the managing partner) refueled guests after skiing and other workouts with a flavorful lower-fat chili. It keeps well in a cooler if you want to make it at home.

   2 tablespoons safflower oil or olive oil
   1 medium onion, chopped
   1 yellow or orange bell pepper, chopped
   1 large poblano chile, chopped
   2 garlic cloves, minced
   1 pound ground turkey
   2 cans (each 28 ounces) diced tomatoes
   2 cans (each 15 ounces) black beans, preferably reduced-sodium, drained and rinsed
   3 tablespoons tomato paste
   3 tablespoons chili powder
   2 teaspoons ground cumin
1½ teaspoons agave nectar or 2 teaspoons sugar
     Juice of 1 lime
     Kosher salt (optional)
     Shredded cheddar cheese and chopped cilantro (optional)

AT HOME OR IN CAMP

1. Heat oil in a large pot over medium-high heat. Sauté onion, bell pepper, chile, and garlic, stirring often, 5 to 6 minutes. Add turkey, increase heat to high, and cook, stirring often and breaking meat into chunks, until it's no longer pink, 4 to 5 minutes.

2. Stir in tomatoes, beans, tomato paste, chili powder, cumin, and agave. Cover and bring chili to a boil, stirring often. Reduce heat and simmer, stirring occasionally, until flavors are blended, 45 minutes to 1 hour. Stir in lime juice. If you like, add salt to taste and serve with cheese and cilantro.

MAKE AHEAD *Up to 3 days, chilled; reheat to serve.*

PER 1½-CUP SERVING 251 Cal., 31% (79 Cal.) from fat; 16 g protein; 8.8 g fat (1.6 g sat.); 27 g carbo (6.4 g fiber); 538 mg sodium; 45 mg chol. **GF/LC**

CHICKEN ENCHILADA NACHO BOWLS

Serves 4 | 20 minutes at home; 20 minutes in camp

This Mexican spin on the campground favorite Frito pie is a guaranteed crowd-pleaser.

CHICKEN AND SAUCE
   1 medium onion, cut into semicircles
   1 tablespoon olive oil
   1 can (10 ounces) enchilada sauce
   1 cup canned crushed tomatoes
   1 can (15 ounces) reduced-sodium black beans, drained and rinsed
   1 teaspoon dried Mexican oregano
   1 canned chipotle chile, minced
   1 tablespoon packed light brown sugar
   2 cups shredded cooked chicken, such as rotisserie
NACHOS
   8 ounces tortilla chips, coarsely crushed
1¼ cups shredded cheddar cheese
   2 cups shredded lettuce
   ½ cup cilantro sprigs
     Lime wedges and hot sauce

AT HOME

1. Make sauce: Sauté onion in oil in a large frying pan over medium-high heat until softened, about 7 minutes. Add enchilada sauce, tomatoes, beans, oregano, chile, and sugar and cook, stirring occasionally, until the mixture is hot and slightly reduced, 4 minutes. Stir in chicken. Let cool, then transfer to a container with a lid or a resealable plastic bag and chill.

IN CAMP

2. Assemble nachos: Reheat chicken mixture in a pan on a camp stove. Divide tortilla chips among bowls and top with chicken mixture, cheese, lettuce, and cilantro. Serve with lime wedges and hot sauce.

MAKE AHEAD *Chicken and sauce, up to 1 month, frozen. Thaw in cooler.*

PER SERVING 772 Cal., 43% (332 Cal.) from fat; 45 g protein; 36 g fat (8.4 g sat.); 70 g carbo (13 g fiber); 1,559 mg sodium; 38 g chol.

CHICKEN ENCHILADA
NACHO BOWLS

COWBOY HOT DOGS

Serves 4 | 30 minutes in camp, plus 20 to 60 minutes for the fire

With several toppings, including caramelized onions, bacon, and barbecue sauce, these can be customized for a range of diners, from those who like their dogs plain to those who want them fully loaded.

    1 tablespoon olive oil
    1 large yellow onion, cut into semicircles
    4 bison* or other hot dogs
    4 potato hot dog buns
      About 6 tablespoons mayonnaise
      About 2 tablespoons spicy brown mustard,
      such as Gulden's
      About 4 tablespoons barbecue sauce
    ½ cup shredded white cheddar cheese
    6 slices cooked bacon, crumbled

1. Heat oil in a large frying pan over medium heat on a camp stove, or over a charcoal- or wood-fired grill heated to medium (about 350°; you can hold your hand 5 inches above cooking grate only 5 to 7 seconds). Add onion and cook until deep golden and very tender, stirring frequently, about 20 minutes.

2. Meanwhile, if you don't already have it going, heat a charcoal- or wood-fired grill to medium (see step 1). Grill hot dogs until slightly charred all over, about 6 minutes, turning occasionally. Add buns and grill, turning frequently, until warmed and lightly charred, about 3 minutes.

3. Spread buns with mayonnaise and drizzle with mustard and barbecue sauce. Set hot dogs in buns.

4. Sprinkle cheese on top, followed by caramelized onions and bacon.

*Find bison hot dogs at well-stocked grocery stores and online.

PER SERVING 633 Cal., 63% (399 Cal.) from fat; 17 g protein; 44 g fat (13 g sat.); 9.5 g carbo (1.7 g fiber); 1,111 mg sodium; 69 mg chol.

EGG SALAD SANDWICHES with HERB MAYO

Serves 4 or 5 | 35 minutes at home; 15 minutes in camp

We've given the familiar sandwich a gourmet makeover with briny olives, radishes for crunch, and plenty of parsley and green onions in the mayonnaise. You want bread or rolls on the softer side, so the filling won't squoosh out the sides when you cut the sandwiches. Still, keep the napkins handy.

    6 large eggs
    ⅔ cup mayonnaise
    ⅓ cup thinly sliced green onions
    ½ cup chopped flat-leaf parsley
      About ¼ teaspoon *each* kosher salt and pepper
    4 large seeded hamburger buns (13 ounces total),
      split, or 10 slices whole-wheat sandwich bread
    4 to 5 tablespoons drained sliced kalamata olives
    6 radishes, thinly sliced
    1½ handfuls (1½ cups) baby arugula or torn romaine
      lettuce leaves

AT HOME

1. Put eggs in a saucepan and cover with water. Bring to a simmer and cook 12 minutes. Rinse with cold water and let cool. Peel eggs, then seal in a container. In a bowl, combine mayonnaise, onions, parsley, and ¼ teaspoon *each* salt and pepper; transfer mixture to a container with a lid. Chill eggs and herb mayo in a refrigerator or cooler.

IN CAMP

2. Quarter eggs lengthwise. In a medium bowl, gently combine herb mayo and eggs. Spoon egg mixture over bottom half of buns or over half of bread slices. Layer olives, radishes, and arugula on top and add salt and pepper to taste. Cover with tops of rolls or remaining bread. Cut sandwiches in half.

MAKE AHEAD *Through step 1, up to 1 day, chilled. Or up to 3 days: Bring eggs unshelled and ingredients for herb mayo, chilled; combine in camp.*

PER SERVING 449 Cal., 44% (198 Cal.) from fat; 15 g protein; 22 g fat (4.5 g sat.); 46 g carbo (2.2 g fiber); 884 mg sodium; 262 mg chol. **LC/V**

FOODS
to Forage

There's mystery and the thrill of discovery in foraging for wild foods. When you're out in forest or desert, or along the seashore, foraging makes a great excuse to explore, and it will open your eyes to the beauty of the natural world around you.

Though the following plants grow in many areas and are easy to identify, the number-one rule for foraging is to be positive of what you are picking. Take a guidebook with you if you're unsure. Additional tips: Avoid roadside areas near traffic, places where pets romp, and any area that might have been treated with agriculture sprays. Harvest responsibly, leaving some plants behind to regenerate and to feed wildlife. And when you try a new food, start by eating just a little.

1.
SPRING
MINER'S LETTUCE

This mild, succulent green, which is full of vitamin C, helped keep miners healthy during California's Gold Rush. In forests and near streams, look for plants up to a foot tall. Try leaves, stems, and small flowers in salad with a simple vinaigrette.

2.
SPRING
NETTLES

Herbaceous nettles are excellent sautéed with garlic and chile flakes. Look for the fine-toothed, tapered leaves along streams. To harvest, grab your long gloves, clippers, and a big bag—you'll need them to avoid the formic acid "sting" in the hairs on nettles' leaves and chest-high stalks. Once you've deposited them in a pan, you can relax: Heat deactivates the sting.

5.

SUMMER
HUCKLEBERRIES

Intensely colored and flavored huckleberries come in many varieties and colors, from pink to blue to black. They thrive in high country meadows and forests and even grow at sea level. Shrubs may grow ankle-high to more than 10 feet. If any last past a trail snack, they make the world's best cobbler.

3.

SPRING
NOPALES

The pads of slightly tart, green bean–tasting nopal—aka prickly pear cactus—come armed with spines and barbed, fuzzy dots (glochids), so be ready with thick gloves. Look for the cactus in deserts to more temperate areas. Cut tender young pads above the joint, leaving a stub to regrow. Remove everything prickly with a vegetable peeler or small knife. Slash pads in a couple of places and grill or slice and sauté until sticky juices evaporate. Try nopales with scrambled eggs and salsa.

4.

SPRING
DOUGLAS FIR OR SPRUCE TIPS

The chartreuse tender new growth of these forest trees offers exciting tastes of citrus or resin. Pull the tips from trees and try them infused in vodka or syrup, chopped in salads, or minced and patted onto meats.

6.

SUMMER
SEA BEANS

In salt marshes and on sandy beaches at the high tidemark, mats of crunchy salty succulents called sea beans grow. Cut off the top few tender inches and try sea beans raw as a snack or in salads. (Soak first briefly in water, if you like, to lessen their saltiness.)

PEANUT BUTTER CRANBERRY GO-BARS

Makes 16 | 1 hour, plus 30 minutes to chill, at home

Loaded with good-for-you ingredients, these not-too-sweet bars still taste like a treat, and they'll withstand cold, heat, and being stuffed into a backpack or pocket. Natural peanut butters vary from brand to brand in terms of spreadability; we prefer Laura Scudder's Old Fashioned Nutty Peanut Butter, because it makes a moister, chewier bar.

  Cooking-oil spray
1 cup regular rolled oats
⅓ cup oat bran
3 tablespoons flax seeds
1 cup whole-wheat flour
½ teaspoon each baking powder and table salt
½ cup each chopped roasted salted peanuts, dried cranberries, and finely chopped dried Mission figs
¾ cup natural chunky peanut butter
¼ cup low-fat milk
1 large egg
½ cup honey
  Zest of 1 lemon
1 tablespoon lemon juice

1. Line a 9- by 13-inch pan with plastic wrap, leaving an overhang on the 9-inch sides, and coat with cooking-oil spray. In a large bowl, stir together oats, oat bran, flax seeds, flour, baking powder, salt, peanuts, cranberries, and figs until well blended.

2. In another bowl, using a mixer, beat together peanut butter, milk, egg, honey, lemon zest, and lemon juice until well blended.

3. Add flour mixture to peanut butter mixture and beat until completely blended. Scrape dough into pan and, with wet fingers or a rubber spatula, pat to fill pan completely and evenly (dough is sticky, so you may need to wash your hands a few times). Chill dough until firm, about 30 minutes.

4. Meanwhile, preheat oven to 300°. Invert pan onto a work surface, lift off pan, and peel off plastic. Using a bench scraper or knife, cut rectangle lengthwise, then crosswise, to make 16 bars, each about 1½ inches wide. Place bars about 1 inch apart on a baking sheet lined with parchment.

5. Bake bars until lightly browned and somewhat firm to touch, about 20 minutes. Remove from oven and let cool completely.

MAKE AHEAD *Up to 2 weeks, stored airtight, or 2 months, frozen.*

PER BAR 227 Cal., 40% (90 Cal.) from fat; 7.4 g protein; 10 g fat (1.5 g sat.); 29 g carbo (4.1 g fiber); 160 mg sodium; 13 mg chol. **LC/LS/V**

SESAME DATE BARS

Makes 16 | 1 hour, plus 30 minutes to chill, at home

This bar is rich with the flavors of the Middle East.

Follow directions for Peanut Butter Cranberry Go-Bars (at left), but increase oat bran to 1 cup. Substitute ½ cup **toasted sesame seeds** for the peanuts, 1 cup chopped **pitted dates** for the figs and cranberries, and ¾ cup **tahini** (sesame paste) for the peanut butter; then add 2 tablespoons more honey.

PER BAR 235 Cal., 38% (90 Cal.) from fat; 6.7 g protein; 10 g fat (1.5 g sat.); 35 g carbo (5.2 g fiber); 109 mg sodium; 13 mg chol. **LC/LS/V**

PEANUT BUTTER
CRANBERRY GO-BARS

CANDIED ROSEMARY
HAZELNUTS

CANDIED ROSEMARY HAZELNUTS

Makes 3¼ cups | 45 minutes at home

This addictive nibble comes from chef-owner Jason French of the Portland restaurant Ned Ludd and its adjacent events space, Elder Hall. He serves it with cocktails, and also packs it up for camping trips and bike rides with his family.

- 12 ounces (2⅓ cups) whole hazelnuts
- 1½ tablespoons finely chopped fresh rosemary leaves
- 2 teaspoons smoked sweet paprika
- 1½ teaspoons sea salt
- ¾ teaspoon pepper
- 3 tablespoons unsalted butter
- ⅔ cup sugar

1. Preheat oven to 350°. Spread nuts in a rimmed baking sheet and roast until golden in center, about 15 minutes (break one to check). On a work surface, wrap nuts in a kitchen towel and rub vigorously to remove loose skins. Transfer nuts to a bowl; cover with a towel to keep warm. Line baking sheet with parchment paper and set aside.

2. Combine rosemary, paprika, salt, and pepper in a small bowl; set aside.

3. Melt butter in a 12-inch frying pan over medium heat. Add sugar and 3 tablespoons water. Cook, stirring constantly and scraping down inside of pan, until mixture turns light golden and a haze starts to form (sugar will melt, then clump up, then melt again), 8 to 20 minutes, depending on your stove.

4. Add warm nuts; stir and turn them constantly with a spoon and spatula until syrup is deep golden brown, 2 to 8 minutes. Working quickly, remove pan from heat, add salt mixture, and stir until nuts are evenly coated, breaking up clumps.

5. Carefully spread hot nuts on lined baking sheet. Let cool about 15 minutes, then break apart and cool completely. Transfer to a container with a lid.

MAKE AHEAD *Up to 1 week, stored airtight.*

PER ¼-CUP SERVING 184 Cal., 71% (131 Cal.) from fat; 3.1 g protein; 15 g fat (2.3 g sat.); 13 g carbo (2 g fiber); 139 mg sodium; 5.6 mg chol. GF/LS/V

MONKEY BUSINESS TRAIL MIX

Makes 4⅓ cups | 5 minutes at home

Rascals of every age seem to enjoy this blend of sweet, salty, nutty, and fruity flavors.

- 1 cup each broken banana chips, unsweetened flaked coconut (also called shaved coconut), and dried cherries
- 1 cup salted cocktail peanuts or roasted peanuts with only salt added
- ½ cup semisweet chocolate chips

Mix all ingredients together in a bowl, breaking up any clumps of cherries.

MAKE AHEAD *Up to 2 weeks, stored airtight.*

PER ⅓-CUP SERVING 249 Cal., 62% (154 Cal.) from fat; 5.4 g protein; 17 g fat (7.1 g sat.); 23 g carbo (5.6 g fiber); 37 mg sodium; 0 mg chol. GF/LC/LS/V

S'MORES TRAIL MIX

Makes 4½ cups | 10 minutes at home

The name says it all—now you can enjoy the flavors of the classic campfire treat when you're on the go.

- ⅛ teaspoon *each* fine sea salt and cinnamon
- 1 cup *each* mini marshmallows and salted roasted almonds
- ½ cup dark or semisweet chocolate chips
- 2 cups sweetened graham-cracker-type cereal, such as Golden Grahams

Put salt, cinnamon, and marshmallows in a bowl and mix with your fingers. Add remaining ingredients and mix to combine.

MAKE AHEAD *Up to 2 weeks, stored airtight.*

PER ⅓-CUP SERVING 145 Cal., 53% (77 Cal.) from fat; 3.0 g protein; 8.6 g fat (2.1 g sat.); 16 g carbo (2.0 g fiber); 111 mg sodium; 0 mg chol. LC/LS/V

NEGRONIS

The classic campground cocktail may be whiskey, neat, in a Sierra Club cup, but it doesn't take much effort to stir or shake up a special libation. Add a favorite bar snack made at home, like Candied Rosemary Hazelnuts (page 107), and you're set for the golden hour. And don't forget the kids—the spritzers and Cool Kebabs on page 110 will give them something to enjoy while you kick back.

CAMP

Cocktail

SECRETS

Plan ahead
For no-juice/spirits-only cocktails like Negronis (opposite), it's fine to mix up a big batch and bring it with you. For any drink involving citrus juice, pack fresh fruit; bottled can't compare.

Pack the right gear
We tote a vegetable peeler for making twists, a citrus squeezer, plastic pitcher, and measuring cups and spoons. A cocktail shaker is optional. Pack glassware carefully, or opt for plastic.

Ice is key
Fortunately, most campground stores sell bags of ice. If you are relying on ice from home, plan cocktails for your first night, before the ice starts melting. After that, try sangria (opposite).

MARGARITA 1, 2, 3

Serves 4 to 5 | 10 minutes in camp

We call this timeless yet camp-friendly margarita "1, 2, 3" because it has three ingredients in equal parts and because it goes together in a snap. You'll need some clean ice cubes from your cooler.

- ½ cup lime juice
- ½ cup each Cointreau (or other orange-flavored liqueur) and tequila (preferably silver)
- Lime wedges
- Coarse salt (optional)

Combine lime juice, Cointreau, and tequila in a pitcher or bowl. Rub rim of each glass with a lime wedge, then dip in salt if you like. Fill glasses with ice and lime mixture; garnish with lime wedges.

PER SERVING 131 Cal., 0% from fat; 0.1 g protein; 0 g fat; 9.2 g carbo (0.1 g fiber); 0.7 mg sodium; 0 mg chol.

CINNAMON TEA WITH TEQUILA

Makes 4½ cups; serves 6 | 20 minutes in camp

This cozy, spiced drink comes from photographer Shelly Strazis of Long Beach, California, who serves it to friends around an outdoor fire after dinner. She adds a shot of tequila to each mug, but it's also good virgin.

- 1½ Mexican cinnamon sticks* (or 1 regular cinnamon stick), plus 6 regular cinnamon sticks for garnish
- 2½ tablespoons honey
- 2 to 3 drops almond extract
- ¾ cup tequila (optional)

1. Heat 4½ cups water and the Mexican cinnamon in a saucepan on a camp stove until boiling. Reduce heat and simmer 10 minutes. Remove cinnamon.

2. Stir in honey and almond extract. Pour into mugs. If you like, add about 2 tablespoons tequila and a regular cinnamon stick to each.

*Buy Mexican cinnamon at Latino markets.

PER ¾-CUP SERVING (WITHOUT TEQUILA) 31 Cal., 0% from fat; 0.1 g protein; 0 g fat; 8.4 g carbo (0 g fiber); 0.5 mg sodium; 0 mg chol.

NEGRONIS

Serves 6 | 5 minutes in camp

With its bitter component from Campari, an Italian aperitif, a negroni invites slow sipping, making it the perfect campground happy hour drink. If you didn't pack a cocktail shaker, just fill glasses with ice and stir in 2 tablespoons each gin, vermouth, and Campari.

- ¾ cup each gin, Campari, and sweet vermouth
- 6 strips orange zest (each about ½ inch by 3 inches)

In a large cocktail shaker, combine gin, Campari, and vermouth. Add 1 cup ice cubes and shake or stir until mixture is cold. Strain into 6 glasses. Over each glass, twist an orange zest strip to release its oils and drop into glass.

PER SERVING 210 Cal., 1% (2.0 Cal.) from fat; 0 g protein; 0 g fat; 6.7 g carbo (0 g fiber); 1.5 mg sodium; 0 mg chol.

CAMP COOLER SANGRIA

Makes 8½ cups; serves 8 | 10 minutes in camp, plus 3 hours to chill

If you stir together the ingredients after breakfast, they'll have melded perfectly by happy hour.

- 1 tablespoon sugar
- ½ cup pomegranate juice
- 1 orange, quartered lengthwise and sliced crosswise
- 1 apple, quartered, cored, and sliced crosswise
- 1 bottle (750 ml.) red wine, such as Zinfandel
- ¼ cup each brandy and orange liqueur, such as triple sec or Cointreau
- 2 cups cold sparkling water

1. In a large jar or sealable pitcher (at least 2½ quarts) that fits in your cooler, stir sugar with pomegranate juice until dissolved. Stir in the remaining ingredients except sparkling water. Chill in cooler at least 3 hours and up to 1 day.

2. Pour about ¾ cup sangria with some fruit into each glass and stir in about ¼ cup sparkling water.

PER SERVING 155 Cal., 0% (0.9 Cal.) from fat; 0.3 g protein; 0.1 g fat (0 g sat.); 14 g carbo (1 g fiber); 1.7 mg sodium; 0 mg chol.

FRUIT JUICE SPRITZERS

Makes 9 cups; serves 8 | 10 minutes in camp, plus 3 hours to chill

We riffed on the flavors of sangria to create a refreshing alcohol-free version that's great for both kids and adults.

Follow recipe for Camp Cooler Sangria (page 109), but omit sugar, wine, brandy, and orange liqueur. Add 3 cups **unsweetened grape juice**. Increase pomegranate juice to 1 cup and sparkling water to 3 cups.

PER SERVING 92 Cal., 2% (1.5 Cal.) from fat; 0.7 g protein; 0.2 g fat (0 g sat.); 23 g carbo (0.8 g fiber); 8.5 mg sodium; 0 mg chol.

COOL KEBABS

Makes 18; serves 6 | 15 minutes in camp

Threading snacks on mini skewers makes them fun to eat, and the prep is simple enough that kids can help. The basic idea: Choose a flavor combination and make everything about the same size (¾ inch or so). Each makes enough for 18 skewers; you'll need 5- or 6-inch bamboo skewers or larger ones cut to size.

GRAPE-CHEDDAR

36 green grapes (1 pound total)

36 small cubes cheddar or mozzarella cheese (8 ounces total), cut about the same size as the grapes

STRAWBERRY-PEACH

3 peaches, cut into small chunks and mixed with 2 tablespoons lemon juice

14 medium strawberries (3 cups), hulled and quartered

CAPRESE

54 small mixed yellow and red teardrop tomatoes (12 ounces total)

54 small basil leaves (or torn pieces of larger ones)

54 small cubes fresh mozzarella cheese (11 ounces total) or quartered small balls (⅓-ounce *ciliegine* size; 5 ounces total) fresh mozzarella

CUCUMBER-CHICKEN

9 ounces cooked chicken breast (a large half-breast), cut into small chunks and seasoned with a little salt and pepper

2 Persian cucumbers (7 ounces total), cut into small chunks

Choose a kebab flavor combination and alternate ingredients on 5- or 6-inch bamboo skewers*.

*Find 6-inch skewers at cookware stores and pickonus. com, *or use kitchen scissors to cut larger ones to size.*

MAKE AHEAD *Up to 1 day, chilled airtight.*

PER 3-SKEWER SERVING WITH GRAPES AND CHEDDAR 214 Cal., 57% (123 Cal.) from fat; 8.6 g protein; 14 g fat (9.5 g sat.); 14 g carbo (0.7 g fiber); 245 mg sodium; 41 mg chol. GF/LS/V

NEAR-INSTANT
Appetizers

You're on vacation, so why not splurge on a few fancy ingredients you can set out to nosh on with that afternoon cocktail or spritzer?

Triple-cream brie cheese + dried apricots and cherries

Canned sardines with chile flakes and a squeeze of lemon + crackers

Assorted olives with orange or lemon zest, fennel seeds, and olive oil

Manchego cheese + quince paste

Hummus with zaatar and a drizzle of good olive oil on top + cubes of brine-packed feta cheese + pita bread

Spanish chorizo sausage + Marcona almonds + sliced bell peppers

Small watermelon wedges + lime wedges + chili powder and salt for dipping

Smoked salmon with freshly ground pepper, flake salt, and chopped fresh herbs + crème fraîche + pumpernickel bread

Cook in a Dutch Oven

We'll be the first to admit it: The dutch oven looks intimidating. Squat and dark, it has a hardy pioneer aura to it that can make you feel unworthy, as if you can't possibly use one unless you've trudged the length of the Oregon Trail. But this trusty pot is well worth packing on any car camping trip. It's easier to use than it looks, and is extremely versatile. Above all, it lets you do some campground baking, as in the delicious chocolate cake on page 144.

EQUIPMENT

❏ 4-quart* (10-inch) camp dutch oven (with feet and a flanged lid)

❏ Charcoal briquets (or use hot embers from a campfire, though they're more difficult to control)

❏ Chimney starter

❏ Newspaper

❏ Fire starter or matches

❏ Grilling tongs and gloves

❏ Fire ring

*You can find bigger dutch ovens, but this size works for all the dutch oven recipes in the book.

1. PREP THE FIRE

In a fire ring, fill a chimney starter one-half full with charcoal briquets. Crumple newspaper into bottom of chimney and ignite. Let burn until briquets are spotted gray, about 20 minutes.

2. ARRANGE THE COALS

For baking or simmering, arrange 8 coals in fire ring, on the place where the chimney was, setting them in a circle a little smaller than the dutch oven. For sautéing, arrange a solid layer of coals the size of the pot.

3. START COOKING

Set dutch oven on coals, checking that it's level. Put lid in place. For baking or simmering, arrange 16 more coals in a ring around lip of lid and 2 coals in center of lid (see step 4 photo). For sautéing, don't add more coals. Set extra coals aside to add if recipe directs.

4. CHECK THE FOOD

Lift lid by sliding tongs under handle. To decrease heat, scrape away some fuel. To increase heat or cook beyond 45 minutes, add 5 to 6 new briquets to top and bottom of dutch oven (touching lit ones) every 30 minutes, or ignite them in chimney.

CURRIED COCONUT LENTIL SOUP

Makes 7 cups; serves 4 | 15 minutes at home; 40 minutes in camp

With a creamy texture and loads of flavor, this soup tastes complex but goes together with very little effort in camp, because you start by creating a soup kit at home. Be sure to pack a can opener for the coconut milk.

SOUP KIT

   1 tablespoon vegetable oil

   1 tablespoon regular or hot curry powder

1½ teaspoons ground ginger

   1 teaspoon each cumin seeds and kosher salt

¼ to ½ teaspoon red chile flakes

½ teaspoon garlic powder

½ cup chopped sun-dried tomatoes (dry packed)

1½ cups red lentils, debris sorted out

   1 can (14 ounces) coconut milk

   1 quart reduced-sodium vegetable broth

   1 medium onion

IN COOLER

   1 small bunch cilantro

AT HOME

1. Assemble soup kit: Seal oil in a small container with a snug lid, such as an empty spice jar. Seal spices and salt in a second container. Put dried tomatoes in a small resealable plastic bag and lentils in another. Bundle together with remaining kit ingredients.

IN CAMP

2. Add some water to bag with lentils, hold closed, and shake to rinse lentils. Gently pour water from bag. Chop cilantro to make about ½ cup and chop onion.

3. In a large saucepan (at least 3 quarts), heat oil over medium-high heat on a camp stove. Add onion and cook, stirring often, until golden, 5 to 10 minutes. Stir in spice mix and cook until fragrant, 15 to 30 seconds. Add vegetable broth, coconut milk, tomatoes, lentils, and half of chopped cilantro. Cover and bring to a simmer over high heat, stirring occasionally. Reduce heat and simmer, stirring every so often, until lentils fall apart and are tender, 15 to 20 minutes.

4. Stir in about ½ cup water for a thinner texture, or leave soup thick. Spoon soup into bowls and sprinkle with remaining chopped cilantro.

PER SERVING 537 Cal., 45% (240 Cal.) from fat; 23 g protein; 27 g fat (19 g sat.); 57 g carbo (13 g fiber); 1,102 mg sodium; 0 mg chol. **GF (WITH GF BROTH)/VG**

BAILOUT

Foods

It can happen: the monster hike, the drizzly evening, or just the comfort of feet propped up around the fire, leaving the camp cooks ... disinclined to cook. Just in case, be ready with a few instant meals (which, fortunately, keep getting better in quality). Before you leave town, hit the grocery store for items to which you simply add boiling water: packs of miso *or* ramen soup, *and cups of* quinoa *and other grain bowls and the like. And swing by an outdoor store for a couple of* packaged camp meals. *If the camping gods unleash a true downpour, head to the tent for a cold picnic dinner of* fancy cheese, salami, crackers, and dried fruit. *And don't forget the* wine.

PAN-SEARED NEW YORK STEAK and MUSHROOMS

Serves 4 | 40 minutes in camp

Even if you're a beginning camper, you can pull off this four-star dish made on the camp stove. A bonus: The mushrooms, steak, and sauce all cook in the same pan, which makes cleanup a snap.

- 1 pound cremini mushrooms
- 1¼ teaspoons each kosher salt and pepper
- 2 boneless New York strip steaks (each 12 to 16 ounces)
- 2 teaspoons fresh thyme leaves, plus a handful of thyme sprigs
- 3 tablespoons olive oil, divided
- ½ cup dry red wine
- ¼ cup salted butter

1. Swish mushrooms in a bowl of water to clean, and trim any tough stem ends. Cut into halves, or quarter if large. Combine salt and pepper in a small bowl. Sprinkle steaks all over with 2 teaspoons thyme and half of salt mixture, pressing seasonings into meat.

2. Heat 2 tablespoons oil in a large cast-iron skillet over medium-high heat on a camp stove. Add mushrooms, thyme sprigs, and remaining salt mixture. Cook, stirring often, until mushrooms are tender and browned, 14 to 20 minutes. Transfer to a bowl; tent with foil.

3. Heat remaining 1 tablespoon oil in pan over medium-high heat. Cook steaks on both sides, turning once, until browned and done the way you like (cut to test), 8 to 14 minutes total for medium-rare. Transfer steaks to a cutting board and tent with foil.

4. Discard fat from pan. Pour wine into the same pan and cook until reduced to 2 to 3 tablespoons (don't reduce further, or sauce may separate), 1 to 2 minutes. Whisk in butter until melted and blended. Cut steaks in half and set on plates. Drizzle with sauce and serve with mushrooms.

PER SERVING 469 Cal., 59% (276 Cal.) from fat; 41 g protein; 31 g fat (12 g sat.); 6 g carbo (0.9 g fiber); 645 mg sodium; 117 mg chol. **GF/LC**

FANCY

Camp Dinner

A little-known but important rule of a successful camping trip is to serve at least one truly special dinner—something that seems as if it might be impossible to prepare in a campground but is, in fact, surprisingly doable. This will be the meal you'll talk about for many trips to come. Two options that cook right on your camp stove: the pan-seared steaks *(at left), served with sautéed mushrooms and a simple red wine sauce, and the* Paella-Style Chicken and Rice *(page 122), which has all the flavors of paella but takes a fraction of the work.*

RIB-EYE STEAK with PISTACHIO BUTTER and ASPARAGUS

Serves 4 | 10 minutes at home; 30 minutes in camp

Flavorful and generously marbled, rib-eye makes a great splurge meal, particularly when topped with a distinctively flavored butter. If you can't find unsalted pistachios, use unsalted butter to balance the salty nuts. The amount of pistachio butter is generous; if you like, turn the asparagus in some of it right after the spears come off the grill, and top steaks with the rest.

  ¼ cup shelled, roasted unsalted pistachios
  1 cup arugula
  ¼ cup salted butter, softened
  2 boneless rib-eye steaks (each about 12 ounces)
  1 pound asparagus, trimmed
  2 tablespoons olive oil
  1½ teaspoons each kosher salt and pepper

AT HOME

1. Whirl pistachios and arugula in a food processor until minced. Add butter and whirl until smooth, scraping down inside of bowl as needed. Transfer to a small container and chill.

IN CAMP

2. Heat a charcoal- or wood-fired grill to high (450° to 550°; you can hold your hand 5 inches above cooking grate only 2 to 4 seconds).

3. Coat steaks and asparagus with oil and season with salt and pepper. Grill steaks, turning once, until done the way you like, 6 to 15 minutes for medium-rare. Grill asparagus in last few minutes, turning once, until tender-crisp.

4. Transfer everything to a cutting board, dollop steaks with butter, and tent with foil. Let rest for 5 minutes. Slice steaks and serve with asparagus.

MAKE AHEAD *Pistachio butter, up to 1 week, chilled.*

PER SERVING 506 Cal., 66% (334 Cal.) from fat; 38 g protein; 37 g fat (16 g sat.); 5.2 g carbo (2.3 g fiber); 727 mg sodium; 172 mg chol. **GF**

SAUSAGE and BEAN DUTCH OVEN STEW

Serves 6 | 1 hour in camp

Quick to throw together, this hearty dish uses cooked sausages. If you want to make it with uncooked sausages, cook them separately for a few minutes before adding the other ingredients.

  2 cans (15.5-ounce size) each cannellini beans and chickpeas (garbanzos), drained and rinsed
  ⅓ cup olive oil
  1 tablespoon chopped fresh rosemary leaves
  ½ red bell pepper, sliced
  ½ yellow bell pepper, sliced
  1 poblano chile, sliced
  4 medium garlic cloves, chopped
  1½ pounds cooked Italian sausages, such as Saag's or Aidells, cut into 1-inch chunks
  ¼ cup fresh oregano leaves

1. Prepare a fire (see "How to Cook in a Dutch Oven," page 112). Combine ingredients except oregano with ¾ cup water in a 4- or 6-quart (10- or 12-inch) camp dutch oven. Cover.

2. Arrange coals for sautéing. Cook stew, checking pot and stirring every 10 to 15 minutes, and adding more water if stew gets dry, until peppers soften and sausages swell, 30 to 45 minutes. Serve with oregano sprinkled on top.

PER SERVING 490 Cal., 44% (216 Cal.) from fat; 32 g protein; 24 g fat (4.5 g sat.); 37 g carbo (12 g fiber); 804 mg sodium; 87 mg chol. **GF/LC**

RIB-EYE STEAK with PISTACHIO BUTTER and ASPARAGUS

ZAATAR and LEMON
GRILLED CHICKEN

ZAATAR and LEMON GRILLED CHICKEN

Serves 4 | 10 minutes at home; 25 minutes in camp,
plus 20 to 60 minutes for the fire

Put the Mediterranean seasoning blend called zaatar *to
work to give camp chicken a complex flavor with minimal
ingredients. You can start marinating the chicken at
home, and even freeze it ahead.*

- ½ cup olive oil
- 2 teaspoons each lemon zest and minced garlic
- ¼ cup *each zaatar** and lemon juice
- 1½ teaspoons kosher salt
- ½ teaspoon pepper
- 8 chicken thighs with skin (each 6 to 8 ounces)
- 2 lemons, each cut into 4 wedges
- 2 bunches green onions, ends trimmed

AT HOME

1. In a large bowl, whisk together oil, lemon zest,
garlic, zaatar, lemon juice, salt, and pepper. Add
chicken and turn to coat. Transfer chicken and
marinade to a resealable plastic bag and seal. Chill
in a refrigerator or cooler.

IN CAMP

2. Heat a charcoal- or wood-fired grill to medium
(about 350°; you can hold your hand 5 inches above
cooking grate only 5 to 7 seconds).

3. Grill chicken, turning every 5 to 8 minutes, until
well browned and cooked through, 20 to 30 minutes
total; watch for flare-ups and move chicken to a
cooler spot if needed. During last few minutes, grill
lemon wedges and onions, turning once, just until
grill marks appear. Serve with chicken.

**Find in the spice aisle of well-stocked grocery stores and
at worldspice.com.*

MAKE AHEAD *Through step 1, up to 1 day, chilled, or up
to 2 weeks, frozen; thaw in cooler.*

PER SERVING 769 Cal., 58% (446 Cal.) from fat; 70 g protein; 50 g fat
(13 g sat.); 7.9 g carbo (2.4 g fiber); 390 mg sodium; 255 mg chol. **LS**

GRILLED MEDITERRANEAN VEGETABLE SANDWICHES

Serves 4 | 30 minutes in camp

Sunset *reader Rebecca Jansen of Snohomish, Washington, won us over with this Mediterranean-inspired
vegetable sandwich that cooks on the grill. It's great for
lunch or dinner.*

- ¼ cup mayonnaise
- 2 garlic cloves, minced
- ½ teaspoon lemon juice
- 2 small zucchini, thinly sliced lengthwise
- 2 portabella mushrooms, sliced ¼ inch thick
- 1 eggplant (14 ounces), sliced ¼ inch thick
- 2 tablespoons olive oil
- ½ teaspoon kosher salt
- ¾ of a 1-pound ciabatta loaf, split horizontally
- 2 ounces feta cheese, crumbled (½ cup)
- 2 medium tomatoes, sliced
- 2 cups baby arugula

1. Heat a charcoal- or wood-fired grill to high (450° to
550°; you can hold your hand 5 inches above cooking
grate only 2 to 4 seconds). Meanwhile, mix together
mayonnaise, garlic, and lemon juice; set aside.

2. Brush zucchini, mushrooms, and eggplant with
oil and sprinkle with salt. Grill, turning once, until
softened and grill marks appear, about 3 minutes.
Grill bread cut side down just until grill marks start
to appear, 2 minutes.

3. Cut each half of loaf into 4 pieces. Spread bottoms
with mayo mixture and smear tops with cheese.
Make sandwiches with vegetables, tomatoes, and
arugula.

PER SANDWICH 421 Cal., 65% (273 Cal.) from fat; 10 g protein; 30 g
fat (6.5 g sat.); 31 g carbo (6 g fiber); 711 mg sodium; 18 mg chol. **LC/V**

PAELLA-STYLE CHICKEN and RICE

Serves 6 to 8 | 15 minutes at home; 1½ hours in camp

The Spanish rice dish paella usually requires a fire and a special pan; this version features the traditional seasonings of saffron and smoked paprika, but cooks on the camp stove in a pasta-size pot. You can get a jump on the prep before you leave home. If you pack the chicken and shrimp frozen in the cooler, they'll keep longer.

- 1 small onion
- 1 green bell pepper
- 1 cup pimiento-stuffed green olives
- ½ pound Spanish chorizo or andouille sausage
- 1½ pounds boned, skinned chicken thighs
- 1¼ teaspoons kosher salt, divided
- 2½ teaspoons smoked sweet paprika, divided
- 3 tablespoons olive oil, divided
- 1 fennel bulb with feathery greens
- 3 large garlic cloves, minced
- ¼ teaspoon saffron threads
- 1 can (14½ ounces) diced tomatoes
- 2 cups Arborio rice
- ¾ cup Spanish fino sherry or other dry sherry
- 1 can (14½ ounces) reduced-sodium chicken broth
- 8 ounces thawed frozen shelled and deveined cooked small shrimp (70 to 110 per pound)

AT HOME

1. Chop onion and bell pepper and put in an airtight container. Put olives in a container. Thinly slice chorizo and package airtight. Cut each chicken thigh into 3 pieces, toss with ½ teaspoon *each* salt and paprika, and package airtight. Chill ingredients.

IN CAMP

2. Heat 1 tablespoon oil in a 6-quart pot over medium-high heat on a camp stove. Add chorizo and sauté until browned, about 5 minutes. Transfer to a plate with a slotted spoon.

3. Brown half of chicken at a time in pot, turning over once, until cooked through, 6 to 8 minutes per batch. Transfer to a second plate.

4. Meanwhile, trim ends from fennel and reserve feathery tops. Halve fennel lengthwise. Cut out core in a V and thinly slice bulb.

5. Add the remaining 2 tablespoons oil to pot along with fennel slices, onion, and bell pepper. Sauté until fennel softens, 7 to 8 minutes. Stir in garlic, remaining ¾ teaspoon salt, remaining 2 teaspoons paprika, and the saffron and cook until fragrant and sizzling, about 1 minute. Add tomatoes; cook, stirring, until thick, about 5 minutes.

6. Add rice and stir until coated, then stir in 1 cup water, the sherry, broth, olives, and chorizo. Cover and bring to a boil over high heat. Reduce heat and simmer until rice is tender and liquid is almost absorbed, about 25 minutes.

7. Arrange chicken with any juices and shrimp over rice. Cook, covered, until shrimp and chicken are hot, about 5 minutes. Chop fennel fronds and scatter on top.

MAKE AHEAD *Through step 1, up to 2 days, chilled.*

PER 2-CUP SERVING 463 Cal., 44% (204 Cal.) from fat; 33 g protein; 23 g fat (5.8 g sat.); 29 g carbo (2 g fiber); 1,155 mg sodium; 144 mg chol. **LC**

ITALIAN-STYLE HOBO BUNDLES

Serves 6 | 1½ hours in camp, including time for the fire

The tried-and-true meal in a foil pouch gets a serious upgrade in this version seasoned with fresh herbs and parmesan. For a head start, make the meatballs at home (see Make Ahead, at right). You'll need heavy-duty foil.

About 5 tablespoons olive oil, divided

⅓ cup dried Italian-style bread crumbs

⅓ cup milk

½ cup grated parmesan cheese, plus shredded parmesan for serving

3 tablespoons chopped flat-leaf parsley, plus whole leaves for serving

3 tablespoons chopped fresh basil, plus whole leaves for serving

1 teaspoon kosher salt, divided

1 teaspoon pepper, divided

1 tablespoon chopped Calabrian chiles or ¼ teaspoon cayenne, plus more chiles (optional) for serving

1 pound ground turkey (preferably thigh meat)

1 pound ground Italian sausage (chicken or turkey, preferably bulk)

2 pounds small red potatoes, cut into 1- to 1½-inch chunks or halves

1 large onion, cut into slim wedges

4 medium carrots, sliced diagonally

4 teaspoons cornstarch

1. Heat a charcoal-fired* or wood-fired grill to medium (about 350°; you can hold your hand 5 inches above cooking grate only 5 to 7 seconds). Cut sheets of heavy-duty foil into six 18-inch squares. Brush or rub center of each with a little oil; set on work surface.

2. In a large bowl, combine bread crumbs, milk, grated parmesan, chopped parsley and basil, ½ teaspoon *each* salt and pepper, and the chopped Calabrian chiles. Add ground turkey and sausage (squeeze it from casings if it's in links). Stir until well blended, then shape into 18 balls, setting 3 meatballs in the center of each foil square. Divide potatoes, onion, and carrots among squares.

3. In a small bowl, combine remaining ¼ cup oil, ⅓ cup water, the cornstarch, and remaining ½ teaspoon *each* salt and pepper; spoon over ingredients on foil, stirring sauce as you go.

4. With each square, bring 2 opposite sides of foil together across the middle and fold to make a seam 1 inch wide. Fold seam on itself again, then fold it flat on packet. Fold ends on themselves about 1 inch, then repeat to seal securely.

5. Set packets on grill and cook, turning over with grilling tongs every 10 minutes, until vegetables are tender and meatballs are cooked through, about 30 minutes (to check, open with a knife).

6. Protecting yours hands with grilling gloves, open packets (or snip off ends of foil with scissors) and scoop food onto plates. Snip or tear whole parsley and basil leaves on top and serve with more chiles and shredded parmesan.

For a charcoal fire, ignite a full chimney of briquets once you've made the meatballs, and let burn until covered with ash. Spread beneath cooking grate, then ignite a second chimney to add during cooking if needed to maintain a medium fire (see step 1 for how to measure heat); cooking may take up to 1 hour.

MAKE AHEAD *Freeze meatballs (step 2) on baking sheets lined with parchment paper until solid, then transfer to resealable plastic bags, double-lined with parchment. Pack frozen in your cooler and thaw before cooking (takes 1 to 2 days). You can also chill packets (through step 4) in cooler up to 6 hours.*

PER SERVING 530 Cal., 45% (239 Cal.) from fat; 35 g protein; 27 g fat (6.2 g sat.); 38 g carbo (4.6 g fiber); 1,079 mg sodium; 124 mg chol.

GRILLED SALMON PACKETS

Serves 4 | 20 minutes in camp, plus 20 to 60 minutes for the fire

Ranch dressing makes a surprising and delicious sauce for salmon. The recipe is adapted from one created by Outstanding in the Field, a California-based company that serves open-air feasts. To go with the fish, grill zucchini halves and packets of boiled potatoes with a little olive oil.

    4 sockeye salmon fillets (with or without skin; each 5 to 6 ounces and about ¾ inch thick), thawed if frozen and any liquid drained
    About 3 tablespoons olive oil
  ½ teaspoon each kosher salt and pepper
    About ¾ cup Homemade Ranch Dressing (recipe at right), divided
    Fresh dill sprigs

1. Heat a charcoal- or wood-fired grill to medium (350°; you can hold your hand 5 inches above cooking grate only 5 to 7 seconds).

2. Meanwhile, cut four sheets of foil, each about 1 by 1½ feet. Set a salmon fillet on center of each. Drizzle each salmon fillet with about 2 teaspoons oil, sprinkle with salt and pepper, and turn to coat. Then drizzle each with 2 tablespoons dressing and turn to coat, ending with skin or skinned side down. Seal foil lengthwise, folding edges together several times. Roll up ends of packets close to fish.

3. Set packets on cooking grate folded side down and cook until you hear sizzling, about 3 minutes. Turn packets over, using grilling tongs. Carefully slit foil lengthwise with a small knife. Steady packets with knife and open them up with tongs, without spilling sauce. Cook until fish is just cooked through, 1 to 7 minutes more.

4. Tear dill sprigs into pieces and scatter over fish. Serve with more dressing on the side.

PER SERVING 432 Cal., 61% (263 Cal.) from fat; 34 g protein; 29 g fat (4.7 g sat.); 6.8 g carbo (0.2 g fiber); 562 mg sodium; 103 mg chol. **LC**

HOMEMADE RANCH DRESSING

Makes 1⅔ cups | 10 minutes at home

Like the salmon (at left), this fresh version of the much-loved salad dressing comes from Outstanding in the Field. For a recipe to serve with greens, see page 137.

  ¾ cup each mayonnaise and buttermilk
  ¼ cup lemon juice
  ¾ teaspoon each kosher salt and pepper
  3 tablespoons chopped fresh dill or 1 tablespoon dried dill

In a bowl, whisk all ingredients to blend (or shake them in a sealed jar). Transfer to a container with a lid and chill in refrigerator or cooler.

MAKE AHEAD *Up to 1 week, chilled.*

PER 2-TABLESPOON SERVING 60 Cal., 70% (42 Cal.) from fat; 0.6 g protein; 4.7 g fat (0.7 g sat.); 4.4 g carbo (0.1 g fiber); 199 mg sodium; 4.1 mg chol.

ONE-PAN MAC 'n' CHEESE

Makes 6½ cups; serves 4
30 minutes at home; 20 minutes in camp

Homemade sharp cheddar cheese sauce and smoked paprika bread crumbs give this recipe a massive flavor boost over the boxed version. For the easiest prep in camp, make the cheese sauce and bread crumbs at home and buy pasta that cooks in one pan without draining. (Or cook regular pasta in camp as noted.)

BREAD CRUMBS AND SAUCE

1½ cups fresh ciabatta bread crumbs*
1½ tablespoons olive oil
1⅛ teaspoons kosher salt, divided
    About ¾ teaspoon pepper, divided
¾ teaspoon smoked sweet paprika
¼ cup each salted butter and flour
2 cups each milk and shredded sharp cheddar cheese

PASTA

12 ounces Barilla Pronto elbow macaroni (a one-pan, no-drain pasta)* or regular macaroni

AT HOME

1. Toast bread crumbs: In a large frying pan over medium heat, cook crumbs with oil and ⅛ teaspoon *each* salt and pepper, stirring often, until crumbs begin to crisp, 4 to 5 minutes. Add paprika and cook, stirring, until crunchy, 2 to 4 minutes more. Pour from pan to a bowl and let cool; then seal in a lidded container or resealable plastic bag.

2. Make sauce: Melt butter in a medium saucepan over medium-high heat. Add flour and remaining 1 teaspoon salt and ½ teaspoon pepper; whisk until bubbling and light tan, 1½ to 2 minutes. Add milk and cook, whisking, until sauce bubbles and thickens, 3 to 5 minutes. Remove from heat, add cheese, and whisk until melted. Let cool, then transfer to a lidded container and chill in refrigerator or cooler.

IN CAMP

3. Pour pasta into a 12-inch cast-iron skillet or other large, deep frying pan on a camp stove; add 3 cups cold water. Cook over high heat, stirring often, until all but about ½ cup water is absorbed, 10 to 15 minutes. (For regular pasta, cook in a large pot

of boiling water until just tender. Set aside ½ cup cooking water; drain pasta and return to pot with reserved water.)

4. Add cheese sauce to pasta and bring to a simmer, stirring often. Spoon into bowls and scatter bread crumbs on top.

Whirl a few slices of bread in a food processor to make crumbs. Find Pronto pasta at well-stocked grocery stores.

MAKE AHEAD *Through step 2, up to 3 days.*

PER SERVING 834 Cal., 43% (360 Cal.) from fat; 32 g protein; 40 g fat (21 g sat.); 88 g carbo (3.4 g fiber); 990 mg sodium; 104 mg chol. **V**

PENNE ALL'AMATRICIANA

Serves 4 | 30 minutes in camp

Sunset reader Jane Ingraham of San Marcos, California, suggests using freshly grated parmesan and freshly ground pepper to take this simple but very satisfying dish to the next level.

8 ounces penne pasta
4 ounces pancetta or good-quality bacon, cubed
1 cup chopped onion
1 tablespoon minced garlic
1 large can (28 ounces) diced tomatoes
1 teaspoon each kosher salt, pepper, and red chile flakes
¼ cup grated parmesan cheese

1. Cook pasta according to package directions; drain and set aside, covered.

2. Cook pancetta in a large frying pan over medium-high heat until partly translucent. Spoon off most of drippings. Add onion and garlic; cook, stirring often, until browned, 5 minutes. Add remaining ingredients except parmesan and cook over high heat until juices have reduced by half, about 10 minutes. Add pasta, stir to coat, and transfer to a bowl. Sprinkle with parmesan.

PER SERVING 362 Cal., 23% (83 Cal.) from fat; 14 g protein; 9.4 g fat (3.3 g sat.); 56 g carbo (3.7 g fiber); 856 mg sodium; 13 mg chol. **LC**

CAMP PIZZA with SAUSAGE and FONTINA

Serves 4 to 6 | 45 minutes in camp, plus 20 to 60 minutes for the fire (if using)

Alan Rousseau, a guide with Seattle-based Mountain Madness mountaineering company, came up with this ingenious way to make pizza in a frying pan. You'll need a large cutting board.

 About 3 tablespoons olive oil, divided
 1 baked 10- to 11-inch pizza crust, such as Boboli
 2 onions, halved lengthwise, then thinly sliced
 8 ounces bulk Italian sausage
 ¼ teaspoon kosher salt
 ¼ teaspoon pepper
 1 tablespoon fresh thyme leaves or 2 teaspoons dried
 About ½ cup store-bought or homemade pizza sauce
 1½ cups (6 ounces) coarsely shredded fontina cheese
 2 tablespoons grated parmesan cheese
 1 tablespoon fresh oregano leaves

1. Heat a charcoal- or wood-fired grill to medium (about 350°; you can hold your hand 5 inches above cooking grate only 7 seconds) or use a camp stove and medium heat. Warm a large heavy frying pan until hot, then oil pan all over the inside. Toast pizza crust (cheesy side down, if there is one), pressing down on edges, until it's crunchy and golden on bottom, 4 to 5 minutes. Transfer to a cutting board.

2. Stoke fire with 12 to 15 more briquets if using charcoal. Add 2 tablespoons oil to pan, then the onions, sausage, salt and pepper, and thyme. Cook, stirring often, until onions are soft and medium golden brown, 8 to 12 minutes. Remove pan from heat. Scoop onion mixture into a bowl and wipe out pan with a paper towel.

3. Brush pan with remaining 1 tablespoon oil. Fit pizza crust into pan with toasted side up. Spoon on pizza sauce and two-thirds of onion mixture, followed by cheeses, remaining onion mixture, and oregano. Return pan to heat. Cook, covered with lid or foil, until cheese begins to melt (check underside to be sure it doesn't burn), 3 to 5 minutes.

4. Transfer pizza to cutting board. Tent with foil to melt cheese completely, then slice.

PER SERVING 482 Cal., 49% (237 Cal.) from fat; 21 g protein; 26 g fat (9.2 g sat.); 40 g carbo (2.7 g fiber); 1,023 mg sodium; 62 mg chol. **LC**

CUSTOMIZE
— *Your* —
PIZZA

It's easy to adapt this Camp Pizza with any number of other toppings. Here are a few of our favorites to try.

Pepper-Pepperoni
Pepperoni, sautéed green pepper, shredded mozzarella, and slivered yellow onion

Veggie
Sautéed sliced summer squash and mushrooms with dried basil and shredded mozzarella

French Anchovy & Olive
Caramelized chopped onion with anchovies, Niçoise olives, and parmesan

BBQ Chicken & Bacon
Shredded rotisserie chicken mixed with barbecue sauce, crumbled cooked bacon, slivered red onion, and shredded mozzarella

TROUT with BROWNED BUTTER and CAPERS

Serves 2 | 20 minutes in camp

If you're lucky enough to catch your own trout, you want to be ready to show off its flavors simply, without too much fuss. Nutty browned butter and bright capers fit the bill, and the ingredients for the recipe are ones you can keep on hand for other camp menus. This simple yet exciting recipe came from Jon Severson during his stint as chef at Blue Sky Grill in Denver.

- ¼ cup each flour and yellow cornmeal
  About ½ teaspoon kosher salt
  About ¼ teaspoon pepper
- 1 cleaned, boned whole trout (8 to 10 ounces), head and tail removed*
- ¼ cup salted butter
- 1 tablespoon drained capers
  Lemon wedges and flat-leaf parsley sprigs

1. On a large plate, mix flour, cornmeal, ½ teaspoon salt, and ¼ teaspoon pepper. Rinse trout and pat dry; place in flour mixture and turn to coat.

2. Bring butter to a simmer in a small saucepan over medium heat on a camp stove; remove from heat. Skim off and discard foam with a spoon.

3. Pour 1 tablespoon butter into a large cast-iron skillet over high heat; set aside remaining butter. Place trout, skin side down, in pan and cook until browned on the bottom, 2 to 3 minutes. Turn with a wide spatula, reduce heat to medium, and cook until fish is barely opaque but still moist-looking in center of thickest part (cut to test), 2 to 4 minutes more.

4. Meanwhile, add capers to remaining butter in saucepan and shake pan often over medium heat until capers pop open, 1 to 2 minutes.

5. Transfer trout, skin down, to a plate. Spoon caper butter over fish and garnish with lemon wedges and parsley sprigs. Add salt and pepper to taste.

*If you hooked your own fish, see "How to Clean a Fresh-Caught Fish" at right.

PER SERVING 365 Cal., 65% (235 Cal.) from fat; 17 g protein; 27 g fat (16 g sat.); 14 g carbo (0.8 g fiber); 925 mg sodium; 135 mg chol. **LC**

HOW TO CLEAN A

Fresh-Caught Fish

Make a shallow slit down the length of the belly. Pull out the guts with your fingers, then rinse the fish well. Scale it by scraping from tail to head with a table knife. Rinse again. If the fish is too big for your pan, cut off the head and tail.

CHILI LIME CORN on the COB

Serves 6 | 35 minutes in camp, plus 20 to 60 minutes for the fire

Cooking corn on the cob in its husk minus the silk keeps the kernels moist and adds a nice flavor. The prep is flexible; instead of making the whole dish in camp, you can flavor and wrap the corn at home, or prepare just the butter there. Wherever you prep, you can also fully husk the corn and wrap the ears in foil. The recipe comes from restaurateur and television personality Guy Fieri.

> 4 tablespoons salted butter, at room temperature
> 1 teaspoon finely shredded lime zest
> 1 teaspoon chili powder
>   About ½ teaspoon kosher salt
> ½ teaspoon pepper
> ¼ teaspoon granulated garlic
> 6 ears of corn in husks

1. Combine butter, zest, chili powder, ½ teaspoon salt, the pepper, and garlic in a small bowl or resealable plastic bag. Stir or mush around to combine thoroughly.

2. Pull back husk from each ear without detaching from bottom of cob. Remove as much silk as possible. Spread ears evenly with butter mixture. Fold husks back over ears and tie in place with kitchen string or strips torn from outer husks.

3. Heat a charcoal- or wood-fired grill to medium (about 350°; you can hold your hand 5 inches above cooking grate only 7 seconds). Grill corn until tender and charred, turning often, 10 to 15 minutes. Serve with more salt to add to taste.

MAKE AHEAD *Through step 2, up to 1 day, chilled in a cooler.*

PER SERVING 112 Cal., 39% (44 Cal.) from fat; 3 g protein; 3 g fat (2.5 g sat.); 17 g carbo (2.5 g fiber); 150 mg sodium; 10 mg chol. **LC/LS/V**

SPINACH and ORZO SALAD

Serves 4 | 20 minutes in camp

Tossed with a homemade herb dressing and colorful add-ins, this recipe is a step above other pasta salads.

> 1 cup orzo pasta
> 3 tablespoons each olive oil and red wine vinegar
> ½ teaspoon each dried oregano and dried basil
>   About ½ teaspoon kosher salt
> ¼ teaspoon pepper
> 1 quart lightly packed baby spinach leaves, roughly chopped
> ¼ cup slivered dried tomatoes packed in oil
> 12 pitted kalamata olives, sliced

1. Cook orzo according to package directions on a camp stove. Meanwhile, in a large bowl, whisk together oil, vinegar, oregano, basil, ½ teaspoon salt, and the pepper and reserve.

2. Drain pasta, rinse with water until cool, and drain again. Add to bowl with dressing and gently mix in spinach, tomatoes, and olives to combine. Add more salt if you like.

MAKE AHEAD *Up to 2 hours, at room temperature.*

PER 1-CUP SERVING 315 Cal., 44% (140 Cal.) from fat; 6.9 g protein; 16 g fat (1.7 g sat.); 39 g carbo (4.4 g fiber); 550 mg sodium; 0 mg chol. **VG**

SPINACH and ORZO SALAD

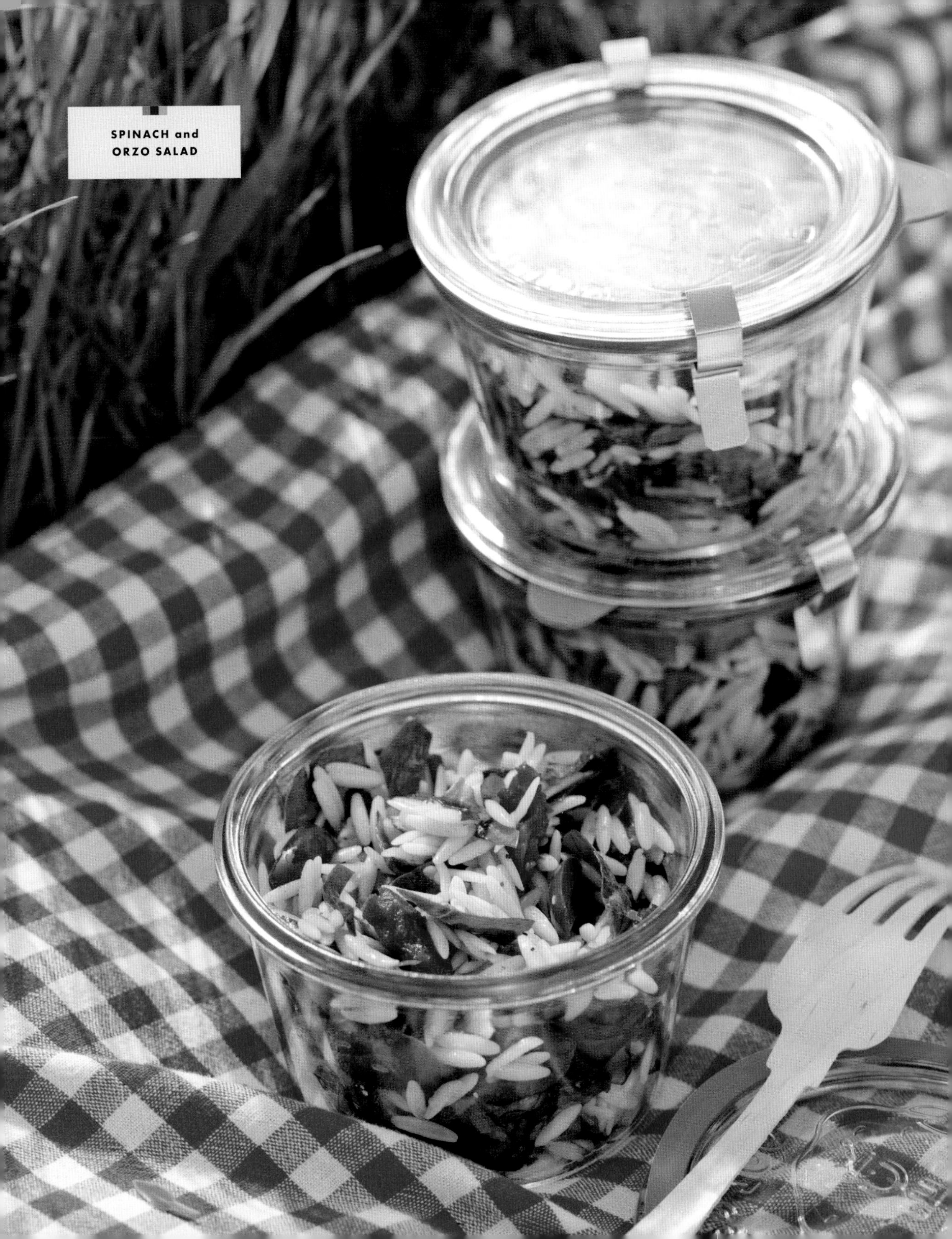

GRILLED POTATO, ONION,
and BACON SKEWERS

GRILLED POTATO, ONION, and BACON SKEWERS

Serves 6 | 1¼ hours in camp, plus 20 to 60 minutes
for the fire

*Crisp-edged bacon, starchy potatoes, and juicy onions
together make an unbeatable side for just about any main
dish. Splurge on top-quality bacon to make it extra-special.
The recipe, by Greg Denton and Gabrielle Quiñónez
Denton of Ox restaurant in Portland, is adapted from their
book* Around the Fire, *with Stacy Adimando (Ten Speed
Press, 2016). You'll need six 14-inch flat metal skewers, or
a dozen 7-inch skewers. If you're using a charcoal fire, start
it when you have about half the skewers threaded.*

- 30 thin-skinned potatoes, no bigger than a ping-pong ball
   (each 1¼ inches wide; 1¼ to 1½ pounds total)
- 1 tablespoon plus ½ teaspoon kosher salt
- 1 medium onion
- ¼ cup extra-virgin olive oil
- ½ teaspoon pepper
- 7 ounces (5 slices) thick-cut bacon, preferably fairly lean,
   cut into 1-inch lengths
- 1 tablespoon chopped flat-leaf parsley

1. Put potatoes in a large saucepan and cover with
water. Add 1 tablespoon salt. Cover, bring to a boil
on a camp stove, then reduce heat and simmer until
potatoes are tender when pierced with a knife, 8 to
10 minutes. Drain, transfer to plates, and let cool
completely.

2. Cut onion into 1-inch chunks and separate into
pieces. In a large bowl, combine oil with ½ teaspoon
each salt and pepper. Add potatoes, onion, and bacon
and toss to coat.

3. On a flat metal skewer, about 14 inches long, thread
2 pieces of onion, a piece of bacon, and a potato,
pressing them close together; repeat until you have
5 potatoes and end with bacon and onion. Thread
5 more skewers in the same way. (Alternatively, use
twelve 7-inch skewers.)

4. Meanwhile, heat a charcoal- or wood-fired grill to
medium-high (about 450°; you can hold your hand
5 inches above cooking grate only 3 to 4 seconds).

5. Grill skewers, turning often, until onion and
bacon have some char to them, 10 to 20 minutes.
Set skewers on a platter and sprinkle with parsley.

PER 14-INCH SKEWER 194 Cal., 57% (111 Cal.) from fat; 3 g protein;
13 g fat (2.4 g sat.); 19 g carbo (2.2 g fiber); 320 mg sodium;
4.8 mg chol. **GF/LC/LS**

HANDS-ON SALAD

Serves 6 | 20 minutes in camp, plus 30 minutes to chill

*If they make it, they will eat it—and likely ask for seconds.
That's the theory behind this salad designed for kids to
swish, tear, peel, and cut, with supervision. Pack kitchen
towels for drying leaves, plastic bags, serrated plastic
knives for young kids or small paring knives for older
ones, and a vegetable peeler.*

- 1 head butter lettuce
- ½ cucumber
- 1 cup cherry tomatoes
   About ¾ cup Homemade Ranch Dressing (page 126),
   or use a little extra-virgin olive oil and salt

1. Cut off lettuce core. Swish leaves in a bowl of water
to rinse. Gently shake leaves dry, then roll in kitchen
towels and put in a plastic bag. Chill lettuce in cooler
about 30 minutes to crisp leaves.

2. Meanwhile, with a vegetable peeler, remove 4 long
stripes of peel from cucumber. Cut cucumber piece in
half lengthwise, then slice crosswise. Cut tomatoes
in half crosswise.

3. Tear lettuce into pieces, dropping them into a bowl.
Add cucumber, tomatoes, and as much dressing as
you like, and toss to mix.

PER SERVING 72 Cal., 60% (43 Cal.) from fat; 1.4 g protein; 4.8 g fat
(0.8 g sat.); 6.9 g carbo (0.8 g fiber); 202 mg sodium; 4.1 mg chol. **LC/LS/V**

EMBER-ROASTED VEGETABLES

Makes 4 cups; serves 4 to 6
30 minutes in camp, plus 1 hour for the fire

While your wood fire grills chicken or another protein on the grate, put the embers to use by cooking some vegetables. You'll need heavy-duty foil.

   4 bell peppers (preferably a mix of red, yellow, orange, and green)
   2 medium onions, peeled and cut in half
   6 tablespoons olive oil, divided
      About 1/2 teaspoon each kosher salt and pepper

1. Build a wood fire in a fire ring (see "How to Build a Campfire for Cooking," page 81), and let it burn down to low flames and embers (1 to 1 1/2 hours).

2. Cut sheets of heavy-duty foil into eight 1-foot squares. Set each bell pepper and onion half on a separate piece of foil, drizzle each with about 1/2 tablespoon oil, and sprinkle with a little salt and pepper. Turn to coat, and scrunch the foil closed.

3. Adjust logs if needed so you can reach embers. Set packets in embers (not in flames) and cook, turning often with long tongs and moving packets around embers as needed, until vegetables are lightly charred (open carefully to check) and feel soft when squeezed, 15 to 25 minutes.

4. Protecting your hands with grilling gloves, open packets. Let vegetables stand until cool enough to handle. Pull off any blackened spots and core and seed peppers. Tear peppers and onions into strips or chunks into a bowl, catching juices. Season vegetables with 2 tablespoons oil and more salt and pepper to taste.

PER SERVING 157 Cal., 77% (121 Cal.) from fat; 1.3 g protein; 14 g fat (1.9 g sat.); 8.5 g carbo (2 g fiber); 131 mg sodium; 0 mg chol. **GF/LC/LS/VG**

KALE SALAD with RED QUINOA and CARROTS

Serves 4 | 25 minutes at home; 5 minutes in camp

Nearly all the prep for this vibrant, satisfying salad can be done at home and the components packed up in your cooler.

   2/3 cup red quinoa, rinsed
   4 small carrots (preferably mixed colors)
   1/3 cup extra-virgin olive oil
   3 tablespoons sherry vinegar
   2 tablespoons pomegranate molasses*
   3/4 teaspoon kosher salt
   1/2 teaspoon pepper
   1 package (5 to 6 ounces) washed baby kale
   1/3 cup crumbled fresh goat cheese
   1/4 cup toasted sliced almonds

AT HOME

1. Cook quinoa according to package instructions, about 20 minutes. Drain any liquid, then spread on a rimmed baking sheet to cool.

2. Meanwhile, very thinly slice carrots on the diagonal. Whisk together oil, vinegar, pomegranate molasses, salt, and pepper in a small bowl.

3. In a medium bowl, combine one-third of dressing with quinoa and carrots, then transfer to a plastic container and seal. Seal remaining dressing in a small container. Pack perishable salad ingredients in a cooler.

IN CAMP

4. Let remaining dressing come to room temperature. In a large bowl, toss kale with dressing, then with quinoa mixture. Divide salad among plates and scatter cheese and nuts on top.

*Find pomegranate molasses at well-stocked grocery stores and Middle Eastern markets.

PER SERVING 367 Cal., 61% (224 Cal.) from fat; 9.1 g protein; 26 g fat (4.8 g sat.); 28 g carbo (5.0 g fiber); 285 mg sodium; 5.2 mg chol. **LS/V**

KALE SALAD with RED QUINOA and CARROTS

PULL-APART
GARLIC BREAD

PULL-APART GARLIC BREAD

Serves 8 | 35 minutes in camp, plus 20 to 60 minutes for the fire

Any time you have a fire going is the right time to add a side of garlic bread to toast on the grill. You want a squishy-soft French loaf—it crisps up well and stays fluffy inside.

> ½ cup salted butter
> 1 tablespoon minced garlic or 2 teaspoons granulated garlic
> 1 loaf soft French-style bread (about 15 inches long)

1. Heat a charcoal- or wood-fired grill to medium (about 350°; you can hold your hand 5 inches above cooking grate only 7 seconds).

2. Meanwhile, in a small saucepan on a camp stove, melt butter with garlic over low heat.

3. Cut two sheets of foil about 1 by 2 feet each. Slice loaf in half lengthwise. From cut side, slice each half crosswise about three-quarters through loaf into 1-inch slices. Set one half-loaf on a sheet of foil. Brush cut surfaces, including between slices, with half of butter mixture. Brush other half-loaf with remaining mixture, then place on top of first half. Lay second foil sheet on top and crimp sheets together to seal.

4. Grill bread on the cooking grate, turning every 5 minutes, until crust is starting to crisp and bread is hot in center (open very carefully to check), 20 to 25 minutes. Pull bread apart to serve.

PER SERVING 275 Cal., 38% (104 Cal.) from fat; 6.2 g protein; 12 g fat (7.3 g sat.); 35 g carbo (1.5 g fiber); 461 mg sodium; 31 mg chol. **V**

CAMP CORNBREAD

Serves 9 | 50 minutes in camp

Warm, buttery cornbread is practically a necessity with a batch of chili or stew, and this dutch oven recipe lets you enjoy it freshly baked. Medium-grind cornmeal gives the bread a rustic texture; if you prefer, you can use a finer grind.

> 1 cup each flour and yellow cornmeal (preferably stone-ground medium coarse*)
> ¼ cup sugar
> 2½ teaspoons baking powder
> ¾ teaspoon table salt
> 2 large eggs
> 1 cup buttermilk (or use dried buttermilk* mixed with water according to package directions)
> About ¼ cup salted butter, melted and cooled

1. Prepare a fire (see "How to Cook in a Dutch Oven," page 112).

2. Combine flour, cornmeal, sugar, baking powder, and salt in a bowl. In another bowl, beat eggs to blend with buttermilk and ¼ cup butter. Pour liquids into flour mixture and stir just until evenly moistened.

3. Scrape batter into a buttered 4-quart (10-inch) camp dutch oven and spread smooth. Arrange coals for baking (see page 113).

4. Bake cornbread until it's golden and pulls from sides of pot, about 25 minutes. Loosen bread with a knife and cut into wedges.

*Find stone-ground cornmeal, such as Bob's Red Mill, and dried buttermilk in the baking aisle.

PER SERVING 204 Cal., 35% (71 Cal.) from fat; 4.9 g protein; 8 g fat (4.3 g sat.); 28 g carbo (1.3 g fiber); 414 mg sodium; 64 mg chol. **LC/V**

CAMPFIRE APPLE CRISP

Serves 6 | 45 minutes in camp, plus 1 hour for the fire

Cooking this homey dessert in your campfire is as simple as moving low-burning logs to create a frame around a bed of embers. Whipped crème fraîche gives the apple crisp a touch of sophistication.

- 3 sweet-tart apples such as Cripps Pink, halved lengthwise and cored
- ¼ cup each flour, softened salted butter, regular rolled oats, and packed light brown sugar
- ¼ teaspoon ground cardamom or cinnamon
- ⅓ cup each whipping cream and crème fraîche
- 1½ tablespoons granulated sugar

1. Build a wood fire in a fire ring (see "How to Build a Campfire for Cooking," page 81) and let it burn down to low flames and embers (1 to 1½ hours).

2. Cut foil into twelve 1-foot squares. Divide into 6 stacks of 2 sheets each and set an apple half on each, cored side up. In a bowl, mix flour, butter, oats, brown sugar, and cardamom with your fingers until evenly moistened with no chunks of butter. Mound an equal amount of topping in each apple cavity.

3. For each packet, neatly fold one stacked corner over apple half, followed by the opposite doubled corner; roll remaining corners snug to fruit to seal.

4. Using long grilling tongs, move logs out to surround the embers that remain in the center of fire ring. Create a flat bed of embers in the center big enough for packets. Remove any flaming wood chunks from ember bed. Set packets topping side up in embers. Cook 15 minutes, turning packets over every 5 minutes with grilling tongs and moving positions in ember bed for even cooking. Transfer a packet to a plate and carefully open to check for scorching; if you see any, adjust fire or positions of packets. Cook packets topping side down without turning until topping is lightly browned, 10 to 15 minutes more.

5. Open packets and let cool a few minutes. In a bowl, whisk together whipping cream, crème fraîche, and granulated sugar until thick. Serve with apples.

PER SERVING 289 Cal., 55% (160 Cal.) from fat; 2.2 g protein; 18 g fat (11 g sat.); 32 g carbo (2.7 g fiber); 63 mg sodium; 50 mg chol. **LC/LS/V**

FRUIT IN Foil

Once you've tried the apple crisp packets at left, here are some more combinations to cook in the embers (for sturdier fruits, and toppings that need to brown) and on the grill over coals (for more tender fruits). Feel free to play with your own ideas too.

Peach Crisp

Swap in peach or nectarine halves for the apples, and add a few blueberries if you like.

Banana Boats

Slit bananas lengthwise and add chocolate chips, roasted peanuts, and a drizzle of caramel sauce. Wrap in foil and warm on a grill.

Raspberry Cake

Wrap up chunks of pound cake with raspberries and warm on a grill. Serve with whipped cream (page 144).

Honey Figs

Drizzle whole fresh figs with honey, top with lemon zest and roasted pistachios, and wrap up; warm on a grill.

DUTCH OVEN DOUBLE CHOCOLATE CAKE

Serves 6 | 10 minutes at home; 1 hour in camp

*Whip up this moist, easy cake in the afternoon, and you'll
find yourself with new campground friends by dinner.*

1½ cups flour
 1 cup sugar
¼ cup dried buttermilk*
¼ cup unsweetened cocoa powder
 1 teaspoon baking soda
½ teaspoon table salt
 1 cup chocolate chips, divided
    About ⅓ cup vegetable oil
 2 teaspoons vanilla extract
    Sweetened whipped cream (at right)

AT HOME

1. Combine flour, sugar, dried buttermilk, cocoa,
baking soda, salt, and ½ cup chocolate chips in a
lidded container or a resealable plastic bag. Pour
⅓ cup oil and the vanilla into a second container
with a snug lid. Cut a circle of parchment paper to fit
the bottom of a 4-quart (10-inch) camp dutch oven.

IN CAMP

2. Prepare a fire (see "How to Cook in a Dutch Oven,"
page 112). Meanwhile, generously oil dutch oven,
line with parchment paper circle, and oil paper. Pour
flour mixture into a medium bowl.

3. When the fire is ready, add oil mixture and 1 cup
water to flour mixture and stir until blended. Scrape
into dutch oven and sprinkle with remaining ½ cup
chocolate chips.

4. Arrange coals for baking (see page 113), using only
14 coals around the lip and 2 in center.

5. Bake cake until a skewer inserted into center comes
out clean, 25 to 30 minutes. Remove lid and let cake
cool at least 15 minutes before cutting into wedges.
Serve with whipped cream.

*Find dried buttermilk at well-stocked grocery stores.

MAKE AHEAD *Through step 1, up to 3 months, the mix
chilled and oil stored airtight.*

PER SERVING 537 Cal., 38% (204 Cal.) from fat; 6.1 g protein; 23 g fat
(7 g sat.); 83 g carbo (3.3 g fiber); 431 mg sodium; 3 mg chol. LS/V

HOW TO

Whip Cream in Camp

*If you're going to the trouble of
making dessert, you might as well go all the
way and add a big dollop of whipped cream.
(You did pack the whipping
cream, some sugar, and a little bottle
of vanilla extract, right?)*

Old-school
In a bowl, whisk 1 cup heavy whipping cream
with 1 to 1½ tablespoons sugar and ½ teaspoon
vanilla extract until thick.

Improv
(for fun, or in case you don't have a whisk)
Pour all the ingredients above into a pint-size
or quart-size canning jar, or into a cocktail shaker.
Attach the lid, and shake-shake-shake until thick.

BANANAS FOSTER
with POUND CAKE

BANANAS FOSTER

Serves 6 | 20 minutes in camp

The quick dessert popularized in New Orleans in the 1950s features bananas warmed in a dark-brown-sugar caramel sauce. It's even better made and eaten outdoors.

- 6 tablespoons coarsely chopped pecans
- 3 tablespoons salted butter
- ½ cup packed dark brown sugar
- 1 teaspoon vanilla extract
- 3 firm-ripe bananas, cut in half crosswise, then lengthwise
- 3 tablespoons rum
  Sliced thawed frozen pound cake, or Ice Cream in a Bag (recipe at right)
  Sweetened whipped cream (see page 144)

1. Toast pecans in a large frying pan over medium heat on a camp stove, stirring occasionally, until golden, about 5 minutes. Pour from pan to a bowl and set aside.

2. Melt butter in pan over medium heat. Add brown sugar and vanilla and cook, stirring occasionally, until bubbling, 1 to 2 minutes. Reduce heat to medium-low. Add bananas in a single layer and cook, turning once, just until warmed, about 2 minutes.

3. Turn off heat (to prevent a flare-up) and stir in rum. Turn stove on to high and cook bananas, stirring gently, until sauce is bubbling and slightly thickened, about 1 minute. Spoon bananas and sauce over cake or ice cream and sprinkle with pecans. Top with whipped cream.

PER SERVING (WITHOUT CAKE, ICE CREAM, OR WHIPPED CREAM) 241 Cal., 41% (98 Cal.) from fat; 1.4 g protein; 11 g fat (4.1 g sat.); 33 g carbo (2.2 g fiber); 47 mg sodium; 15 mg chol. **GF/LC/LS (ALL WITHOUT POUND CAKE)/V**

ICE CREAM in a BAG

Makes 1 cup; serves 1 or 2 | 15 minutes in camp

We don't know what's more fun, watching a few ingredients magically transform into ice cream, or getting to eat the results right from the bag. A bonus: You can take your pick of five ice cream flavors. For each batch, you'll need two resealable plastic bags (1-quart and 1-gallon sizes), plus ice and salt for freezing. If you hand off the ice mixture right after using it, it will still be cold enough to shake a second bag.

- 1 cup half-and-half
- 3 tablespoons sugar
- 1 teaspoon vanilla extract
- 1 tablespoon instant espresso powder, ¼ cup chopped strawberries, 3 tablespoons Mexican Hot Chocolate mix (page 97), or 1½ tablespoons Dutch-process unsweetened cocoa powder such as Droste (optional)
- 2 to 2½ quarts ice cubes
- ½ cup rock salt or kosher salt

1. Pour half-and-half, sugar, vanilla, and espresso powder or other flavoring, if using, into a 1-quart resealable plastic bag. Seal, pushing out air. Shake to mix ingredients. Set bag in a 1-gallon resealable plastic bag and fill about two-thirds full with ice. Add salt and seal bag.

2. Wrap bag in a kitchen towel and shake until ice cream is set, 10 to 15 minutes. Serve immediately, right from the bag or spooned into a bowl.

PER SERVING (ESPRESSO FLAVOR) 239 Cal., 52% (124 Cal.) from fat; 3.7 g protein; 14 g fat (8.6 g sat.); 30 g carbo (0 g fiber); 50 mg sodium; 44 mg chol. **GF/LC/LS/V**

BRING ON

— the —

S'MORES

For dessert on a camping trip, s'mores are essential. But why stick with the tried-and-true grahams, milk chocolate, and poufy marshmallows? Gather a few special ingredients and a little equipment before you leave home. When the stars come out in camp, you'll be ready for some delicious fieldwork around the fire.

S'mores

Ready to play? These updated combinations give you plenty of delicious ways to experiment.

Classic Plus
Graham crackers, dark chocolate, and sliced strawberries

Lemon Meringue Pie
Shortbread cookies and lemon curd

Black Forest
Chocolate wafer cookies and cherry jam

Neoclassic
Digestive biscuits and squares of bittersweet chocolate

The Elvis
Peanut-butter sandwich cookies (twist cookies into two halves), dark or milk chocolate, and sliced bananas

Piña Colada
Coconut cookies and grilled slices of pineapple

Gianduia
Gaufrettes, pizzelle (French and Italian waffle cookies), or wafer cookies and Nutella

Thin Mint
Chocolate wafer cookies and thin after-dinner mints, such as After Eight

BUILD A — Better — S'MORE

Upgrade your ingredients
You'll find any number of fancy options at specialty markets and online, from single-origin dark chocolate to peppermint-flavored marshmallows. (Of course, kids may prefer the regular stuff.)

Make a DIY tray
Unwrapping ingredients and setting them out make it easy to customize the treats. Kids' ingredients can be on one side and more adult ingredients can be on the other.

Extend your reach
The biggest s'mores innovation is a technical one: telescoping forks that let you roast and turn your gooey creation from your camp chair. Find them at camping stores and online.

Marshmallow Animals

Use your stash of camping goodies to make edible marshmallow animals that will be the envy of roasting sticks everywhere. Combine different sizes of mallows with pretzel sticks, nuts, and shredded coconut to create all sorts of wild and domestic beasts. Then when you're done... h/eat 'em up! Tip: If you don't plan on eating your creations, you can use toothpicks to connect the pieces instead of icing. This will cut down on the time it takes to make them.

OWL

YOU'LL NEED
- [ ] Scissors
- [ ] Jumbo, regular, and mini marshmallows
- [ ] White decorating icing
- [ ] Slivered almonds

1. To make wings, squish both ends of a jumbo marshmallow into an oval. Cut the marshmallow's ends off so the wing pieces are ¼ to ⅜ inch thick.

2. To make the body, place a jumbo marshmallow, flat side down, on your work surface. Use icing to attach wings to the sides of the body. Let dry 5 minutes.

3. To make chest feathers, use 9 similarly sized almond slivers. Add icing on the front of the marshmallow body. Starting from bottom and working upward, press to attach 3 rows of 3 almond slivers onto body.

4. To make the face, cut ¼ inch off the end of a jumbo marshmallow. The remainder of the marshmallow is the head. Cut two ¼-inch slices off the end of a regular marshmallow. Press the slices, cut side down, onto the cut side of the face piece. The cut sides will stick without icing. These are the feather rounds behind the eyes.

5. To make eyes, cut a mini marshmallow in half and press halves onto centers of the feather rounds.

6. Glue the head onto body with icing. Hold in place until the icing sets.

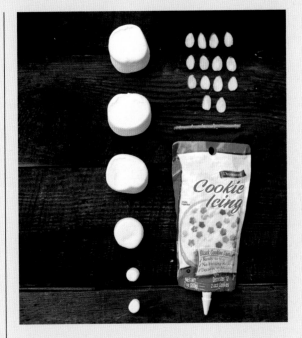

7. Using icing, attach almond slivers to the head as the tufts and beak.

SHEEP

YOU'LL NEED

❑ Scissors
❑ Regular, jumbo, and mini marshmallows
❑ White decorating icing
❑ Bamboo skewer
❑ Pretzel sticks, broken into four 2-inch pieces for each sheep
❑ Slivered almonds
❑ Shredded coconut
❑ Cocoa powder (optional)

1. To make the head, cut a regular marshmallow in half crosswise. Use icing to glue one of the halves to one end of a jumbo marshmallow, lining up the top edges of the marshmallows. Allow icing to dry for 4 to 5 minutes.

2. Once the head is secure, place body of the sheep on its back, belly facing up. Dip the point of a bamboo skewer into water (to prevent stickiness) and use it to poke holes in the body for legs. Push four pretzel pieces about ¾ inch into the holes. Stand the sheep upright.

3. For the tail, cut a mini marshmallow in half and stick it on the sheep with icing.

4. For the ears, attach 2 almond slivers to head with icing.

5. For the wool, spread icing onto sides and top of body and top of head. Sprinkle with shredded coconut. Let dry.

Optional: If you'd like to add eyes, mix a bit of water and cocoa and dip in the tip of a bamboo skewer. Poke tip into the face where you'd like an eye to go. Repeat for other eye.

BISON

YOU'LL NEED
- [ ] Scissors
- [ ] Regular, jumbo, and mini marshmallows
- [ ] White decorating icing
- [ ] Bamboo skewer
- [ ] Pretzel sticks, broken into four 2¼-inch pieces for each bison
- [ ] Cashews
- [ ] Shredded coconut
- [ ] Cocoa powder

1. To make the head, cut a regular marshmallow in half. Use icing to glue one of the halves to the top end of a jumbo marshmallow, lining up the edges of the marshmallows. Allow icing to dry for 4 to 5 minutes.

2. Once the head is secure, place body of the bison on its back, belly facing up. Dip the point of a bamboo skewer into water (to prevent stickiness) and use it to poke holes in the body for legs. Push four pretzel pieces about ¾ inch into the holes. Stand the bison upright.

3. Cut a regular marshmallow in half crosswise, and then put flat side down and cut that circle in half so you end up with two arched pieces.

4. Cut one of the arched halves in half horizontally, so you end up with a smaller arched piece.

5. With icing, glue the large arch in place on the top of the back, just a bit behind the head. Then glue the smaller arch behind the large one. These will form the hump.

6. For the horns, choose a cashew with a pointy tip for the most hornlike appearance; split cashew in half.

7. Use the water-dipped bamboo skewer to poke holes in sides of the head for horns. Fill holes with icing and let sit for 2 minutes before pressing horns in place, with rounded sides facing front. Let sit 3 minutes more.

8. Meanwhile, to make hair, mix ½ cup shredded coconut with 1 tablespoon cocoa powder until coconut is brown. Once the horns are secure, spread icing onto sides and top of body and top of head. Sprinkle with cocoa-covered coconut. Let dry. Lightly dust the whole bison with additional cocoa so it is uniformly colored.

Optional: If you'd like to add eyes, mix a bit of water and cocoa and dip in the tip of a bamboo skewer. Poke tip into the face where you'd like an eye to go. Repeat for other eye.

MINERAL KING VALLEY,
SEQUOIA NATIONAL PARK

CHAPTER 4

Exploring
THE GREAT
OUTDOORS

What's a campout without a little trekking and exploration? BREATHE IN THE FRESH AIR AND TAKE IN THE SCENERY AS YOU HIT THE TRAIL. Snap photos like a pro. Paddle the day away. Here are some ways to have amazing outdoor adventures.

— Let's Go —

HIKING

Camping puts you on the threshold of incredible landscapes—redwood forests, stands of saguaro, and spectacular high country—that are easily explored on day-hikes. There are gentle walks along wildflower-filled meadows and challenging treks with climbs to alpine lakes and glaciers. And the beauty is that you still get back to camp in time for a big dinner cooked over a fire.

Hiking is the most basic of all outdoor activities. After all, what could be more natural than putting one foot in front of the other (albeit maybe 10,000 times on a 5-mile hike)?

MCGEE CREEK AND
THE SIERRA CREST

— Basic —
HIKING GEAR

BE KIND TO YOUR FEET

Go to an outdoors store and shop for a pair of true hiking shoes or boots. Uneven or rocky terrain means that you want the additional traction and support on the trail that less sturdy athletic shoes can't provide. Try to anticipate the kinds of hikes you're most likely to take. There is no point in buying an expensive technical boot designed for trekking in Nepal if you aren't going on anything longer than a three-hour day-hike. For most short hiking needs, light midcut or low-top hiking boots with Gore-Tex or some waterproofing are fine and are typically easier to break in, weigh less, and cause fewer blisters. Reduce your chances of blisters by picking up a few pairs of breathable socks that wick away moisture.

And if you do anticipate daylong outings, or hikes over especially rocky terrain, consider a high-cut hiking boot or a backpacking boot with a stiffer sole for additional ankle support and better stability.

GET A DAY PACK

Keep your hands free and have a place to carry what you need, including a flashlight, maps, and other essentials (see sidebar opposite). Always pack water

SHOE FOR YOU

Get measured
Have a salesperson properly measure your feet rather than guessing the size yourself. (You're also better off getting fitted near the end of the day, by which time your feet have swelled and are closer to the size they'll be as you hike.)

Check the fit
Make sure the shoes are snug everywhere but not tight anywhere. There shouldn't be any areas that rub. Make sure there is some wiggle room with a good thumb's-width between end of your toes and end of the shoes.

Anticipate your needs
Look for a higher cut if you require more ankle support or a stiff outsole for better arch support.

Test before buying
Walk down an incline to make sure that your toes don't press up against the inside of the shoes, then walk around. You want to find any areas of rubbing before you're on the trail.

and snacks so you can refuel on the trail. And don't go out on an empty stomach because you'll get depleted that much sooner.

THINK LAYERS

Bulky clothing lacks the versatility of wearing several layers of thinner, lighter items. You want to respond to conditions by adding and subtracting layers as necessary. Clothing with zippers or buttons give you more options for temperature control than T-shirts and pullover sweatshirts. Stick with moisture-wicking synthetic materials, not cotton, because you're bound to perspire. And having a lightweight, wind-resistant outer shell is always a good idea.

PROTECT YOUR HEAD

Guard against UV rays and keep the sun out of your eyes with a wide-brimmed hat, preferably something lightweight. In colder conditions, hats will reduce heat loss through your head. Even while wearing a hat, apply sunscreen and lip protection.

BRING A COMPASS

For all of the focus on such tech-based navigation tools as GPS systems, when you go camping and hiking, you'll also always want to bring a good old-fashioned compass. And for one good reason: It will never run out of batteries or need satellite signals to work. A basic compass that costs $20 or less can help you get oriented as you set up camp, allowing you to more precisely position your tent for sun exposure. It can also keep you on track during

your trek and assist with stargazing. Many simple compasses attach to a key ring or have a carabiner for a connection to straps or clips on a backpack. For complex navigation, such as trail-less cross-country hiking (not a good idea except for experienced hikers and also prohibited in many parks), you'll need a detailed topo map of the area and a more advanced compass with such features as a sighting notch, magnifier, and an adjustable declination scale.

DAY-HIKE ✓

Checklist

Here are the 10 essentials you need to stay safe and comfortable on the trail.

- ❑ Compass and a good map of the area in a resealable plastic bag to stay water-resistant
- ❑ Sun protection: hat, sunblock, and lip protection
- ❑ Extra clothing, such as a long-sleeved shirt
- ❑ Small first-aid kit, either store-bought or one you put together, including antiseptic and antibacterial wipes, Band-Aids, and antibiotic ointment
- ❑ Space blanket
- ❑ Strike-anywhere matches or a lighter
- ❑ Multi-tool
- ❑ Headlamp or small flashlight
- ❑ Snacks (such as Peanut Butter Cranberry Go-Bars, page 104, or Monkey Business Trail Mix, page 107)
- ❑ Water. The general rule of thumb is to drink ½ to 1 quart of water per hour per person. Check if there is drinking water available on the trail and make sure you carry enough to cover your needs.

Download at Sunset.com/hikinglist

— Hit the —
TRAIL

START SLOWLY

Especially if you haven't been exercising regularly, don't attempt an overly ambitious hike right away. Watch not only the length of the hike but also its elevation gain to avoid climbs beyond your physical abilities. Even if you're a regular hiker, settle into an easy rhythm and let your heart rate begin to increase before picking up the pace. You should be able to carry on a conversation as you hike.

PAY ATTENTION

Look at the surroundings and occasionally turn around to take note of where you are. Pick out a few landmarks along the way—oddly enough, trails can look completely different when seen from the opposite direction, and you'll want to stay oriented. Pay attention to junctions or turns, because you don't want to veer off on the wrong trail. Getting lost is no fun.

KEEP TRACK OF THE TIME

Remember that if you hike two hours in one direction, you have to hike two hours back. In beautiful country, it's easy to just keep pushing ahead, only to have fatigue set in on the return. And you definitely want to be back before dark.

HOW TO

Navigate with a Compass

Many trails are clearly marked, but there may be times you'll have to rely on your map and compass to figure out where you need to go. There are many types of compasses, but one with a transparent base plate, rotating dial, and travel arrow is easy to use with a map.

Spread your map on a flat surface and set the compass level on top. Align the back edge of the compass with your starting point and the front with the travel arrow in the direction you want to go.

Rotate the compass dial until the orienting arrow within the compass and the north end of the compass needle align. Read the number on the dial. This is the bearing and direction you should follow.

Follow the arrow on the compass. Stop and recheck your bearings periodically to make sure you haven't drifted off course.

PENITENTE CANYON,
COLORADO

MOONEY FALLS,
HAVASU, ARIZONA

HIKING
— with —
KIDS

We all know kids today: perpetually tethered to one electronic device or another. The truth is children—yours and everyone else's alike—are really not that different than we were, growing up. But they do face endless distractions that anyone who came of age with CDs, not to mention vinyl records, can scarcely imagine.

Taking the kids camping is a big step in reconnecting them to the natural world. Now get them out on the trail to help them engage their senses and expose them to nature. Leave the earbuds and screens back at camp. Or, if nothing else, show the kids how these devices are not an end in themselves. Find field guide apps for plant, bird, and wildlife identification, then let the kids use technology to better understand what they're seeing (see "Name That Tree, Name That Plant," page 168).

Find appropriate trails
A death march that ends with you carrying one or two kids the last few miles back to camp isn't fun. Start with easy interpretive trails that offer background details about the area. Scout out other trails to determine whether they're appropriate for the family and to identify interesting stops and features.

Get them the proper gear
Sure, they'll practically have grown out of everything by the time you get home from the store. But using a pair of flip-flops on the trail is a guaranteed hiking disaster, so pick up a decent pair of hiking shoes, as well as comfortable clothes. A small day pack that lets the kids carry a few of their own items, such as water and snacks and perhaps an inexpensive camera and small notebook for recording the trip, will also give them a sense of control.

Take a trail with a reward
Keep the kids motivated by letting them know that you actually have a goal, such as a waterfall or view. Once you've reached that destination, they will feel as if they have accomplished something instead of simply trudged through the woods.

Inspire enthusiasm
If you're miserable, they'll be miserable, so put on a happy face. Or at least try.

Indulge their curiosity
Stay flexible and spontaneous. When something grabs the kids' attention, follow their lead. Pack a magnifying glass for close-up looks at bugs and plants. If the stops take too long and you don't reach your destination, so be it.

Hike with a ranger
National and state parks often conduct outings led by rangers. Sometimes just being part of a group will keep children engaged, plus an upbeat, informed guide can bring an area alive.

Set a reasonable pace
Frequent stops for drinks and snacks will reduce the risk of burnout.

Keep everyone together
There are the unlikely mega-hazards—mountain lions and bears (see page 165)—but also a whole host of lesser dangers that can ruin a hike: cactus spines, poison oak, and skunks. Don't let the kids run ahead or fall too far behind. For added insurance, give them a whistle to blow in case you get separated.

WILDLIFE SAFETY
— for Hikers —

Cue the scary music: They're out there. Predators. Grizzly bears that weigh up to 1,700 pounds, black bears that smell food from several miles away, and mountain lions that leap 45 feet in a single bound and take down animals as large as moose. Got your attention yet?

In fact, the odds of humans getting attacked on the trail are quite small, mainly because these animals will probably avoid you long before you notice them. Mountain lions have low population densities and are rarely seen. According to the Mountain Lion Foundation, only 14 mountain lion attacks occurred in California during a nearly 130-year period. Bear encounters are more common and do happen in such prime camping and hiking destinations as Yellowstone and Grand Teton National Parks. They are increasing as more people explore the wilderness. So forgive the scare tactics, but it's better to be safe than sushi. Here's how to be bear- and lion-aware when out in the wild.

GENERAL PRECAUTIONS

NOTICE YOUR SURROUNDINGS. Bears and mountain lions frequently use hiking trails. Check for paw prints, fresh scat, and new claw marks on trees. If you come upon a recently killed deer or elk, leave the area.

MAKE SOME NOISE. Much as you may hate to make a racket, in bear country especially it helps to wear bells, blow whistles, and clap your hands. Particularly in areas of limited visibility, or when rounding a bend, you'll want to signal your presence.

FOLLOW LOCAL RECOMMENDATIONS. Carry bear spray where rangers suggest it and be sure to know how to operate the canister.

GO OUT IN GROUPS. Stick together in groups of four or more and always keep children close.

AVOID DAWN AND DUSK. Predators are more active early and late in the day.

NEVER APPROACH MOUNTAIN LIONS OR BEARS. Yes, it's just common sense, but you'd be amazed at what people will do for a better photograph.

RESPECT
— the —
ANIMALS

When You See a Bear…
LEAVE THE AREA. Forget about the OMGs you'll earn for tweeting a photo of the bear. Try to get away before it notices you. Never make threatening gestures; back away while keeping an eye on the animal, although avoid direct eye contact (bears consider that aggressive behavior). Don't run, either.
WATCH ITS BEHAVIOR. A bear on its hind legs is probably just curious. But stomping feet, clacking jaws, and thrown-back ears are among the signs that this is an angry bear.

If a Bear Attacks…
REMAIN CALM. Granted, easier said than done. But bears will often make a bluff charge, then stop or veer off at the last second.
BLACK BEARS. Fight back (talk about easier said than done). Use anything you can to defend yourself, as you have a better chance of scaring a black bear than a grizzly.
GRIZZLY BEARS. Play dead. Protect yourself by curling up in a ball and clasping your hands against the back of your head and neck to fend off bites.

When You See a Mountain Lion…
WATCH FOR AGGRESSIVE SIGNS. Quiet observation is one thing. But a snarling, stalking lion means trouble.
NO RUNNING. You don't want to trigger the lion's hunting instincts. Maintain eye contact and back up slowly while speaking loudly.
LOOK BIG. You want to look as threatening as possible, by waving your arms or clothing and making a lot of noise. Bending or crouching is the worst thing to do—you'll resemble prey and also leave your head and neck open for attack.

If a Mountain Lion Attacks…
FIGHT THE GOOD FIGHT. Try to stay on your feet. Fists, rocks, and backpacks are all weapons at your disposal to scare off or injure the lion so it leaves you alone.

— Crossing —
STREAMS

If you are planning on hiking in areas where you anticipate crossing streams, consider these tips. And always check with rangers or other local administrators about the rate of water flow before heading out.

GETTING READY

BRING SPARE FOOTWEAR. Carry a pair of hiking sandals or an old pair of gym shoes that you don't care about soaking. Walking through a shallow stream may be safer than tightroping your way across a wet log. Also take along a lightweight microfiber towel to dry your feet.

USE TREKKING POLES. They'll create added stability when crossing a stream and will double as a tool to test water depth.

WEAR CONVERTIBLE PANTS. Wet pants aren't particularly pleasant to hike in and can create drag while crossing a river. Instead, zip off your pants legs and just use the shorts when you go into the water.

ADJUST YOUR LOAD. Especially if you're carrying a day pack, unbuckle your waist belt and loosen your shoulder straps. That way your bag can come off instead of getting soaked and dragging you down if you fall into the river.

TIPS FOR CROSSING

ASSESS THE CURRENT. Throw a branch into the stream to determine the speed of the current. *Never* attempt to cross a fast-moving stream.

LOOK FOR THE BEST SPOT. You want a straight, wide, and shallow stretch for a safe crossing, so be conservative. If you don't see an appropriate place, don't even try to get to the other side. Remember, too, that the point where the trail intersects a river may not be suitable. Better alternatives may be up- or downstream.

CHECK FOR DEBRIS. Branches and logs surging with the current indicate that the stream is running high and strong. The debris could also knock you off-balance.

STICK TO SHALLOW WATER. Don't cross at places where flowing water is above your knees. Any deeper, and you could get knocked down. Wade through deeper water only in a pool with no current.

FIGURE OUT YOUR EXIT STRATEGY. Make sure that you can easily get out of the water on the other side. You don't want to have to scramble up a steep bank where you might fall back into the water.

MAINTAIN YOUR STABILITY. Shuffle your feet and keep at least one of your trekking poles in contact with the stream bottom at all times. You should face upstream and move diagonally while pointed slightly downstream.

COHUTTA WILDERNESS,
GEORGIA

— *Name That Tree,* —
NAME THAT PLANT

Don't be intimidated, but there are an estimated 298,000 plant species on Earth—not that anyone knows for sure. Still, you don't have to be a botanist to identify the major plant species you encounter while enjoying the great outdoors. Just learning a few nature appreciation skills will enhance a hike, and you'll dazzle others when they ask, "Hey, what kind of tree is that?" As they inevitably will. Because, unless you're walking in the desert, there are lots of trees when you're hitting the trails.

HELPFUL TOOLS AND RESOURCES

FIELD GUIDES Designed for specific areas, field guides, such as Sibley or Peterson books, help narrow down the selection of plants and categorize species to speed up identification.

PLANT IDENTIFICATION APPS Save weight in your day pack by downloading digital field guides. *Leafsnap* (which currently focuses on the Northeast U.S. and Eastern Canada) even lets you take a photo of a leaf then use its visual recognition technology to match the image to the right plant. *Audubon Guides* has a series of authoritative field guide apps, including ones for North American trees, wildflowers, and mushrooms, as well as plant and animal guides for select regions.

PARK WEBSITES Especially if you're camping in a national park, check the website for write-ups and photos of prominent plants. The sites vary in detail, but you should be able to find information about plant communities, as well as checklists of what grows in the park. Parks also often provide regular updates on wildflower blooms, fall color display, and other seasonal events. And consult schedules for ranger-led walks that explore local habitats.

MEASURING TOOLS A ruler with both inch and metric increments will help with leaf identification, while a tape measure can provide accurate readings for trunk diameter for those who really, really want to know.

MAGNIFYING GLASS It's often helpful in identification to check leaves or stems for small hairs or spines, and also to look at the vein pattern.

SMALL NOTEBOOK Use this to sketch what you see or to jot down notes if you want to identify a plant later. Include a description of the habitat, color of the flowers, or any other interesting observations.

HOW TO START IDENTIFYING PLANTS

Begin with the most prominent trees in the area where you are camping, then work your way down. Or try to identify the most spectacular or most common wildflowers. It takes a while to understand the structure of plants and the characteristics to look for. Here are some common distinguishing attributes to help identify any plant or tree:

• What are the shape and color of the flower? How many petals does it have?
• Does it have fruit or seeds?
• What does the stem look like?
• How are the leaves or needles arranged? What shape are they?

LEAF TYPE

NEEDLE

SIMPLE

COMPOUND

LEAF ARRANGEMENT

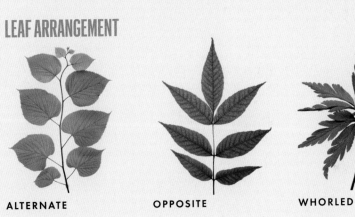

ALTERNATE

OPPOSITE

WHORLED

LEAF SHAPE

UNLOBED

LOBED

TREE BARK

RIDGED

SMOOTH

DEWEY POINT, YOSEMITE

Photograph Like a Pro

Sunset photographer Thomas J. Story knows how to get terrific photos outdoors—whether he's on assignment or on a family trip. His tips:

1. Bring extra batteries and memory cards for your camera, especially if you're out camping someplace where you have no power.

2. Don't bring too much—one camera, one standard lens, and one zoom lens.

3. Do bring a small tripod if you want to try night shots.

4. Capture landscapes in the early morning or late afternoon for the prettiest light. Sometimes you have to get up when it's dark to get to the place you want to photograph before the sun comes up. You almost always need a greater depth of field for landscapes, so stop your lens down at least two stops from its biggest f-stop. Use a lens shade, tripod, and cable release if you can.

5. If you're interested in photographing wildlife, bring one more lens—the longest you have. You'll also need a lot of patience; people who specialize in photographing wildlife can spend hours or days without seeing what they want to photograph.

6. If you are using your phone to take photos, be sure to wipe the lens off periodically. Pano mode works great for capturing wider scenes. And look into apps that let you have more control over camera functions, including setting the exposure manually.

7. But the most important tip is to put the camera down sometimes and relax. You're on vacation—not every moment needs to be recorded.

The Yosemite Valley captured in late afternoon when the quality of light adds warm drama. The use of a polarizing filter improved saturation and decreased contrast, while a lens shade reduced glare.

"Picture This" Photo Safari

A visual scavenger hunt is a fun way to get everyone, including kids, to interact with nature while still being able to use their beloved technology (aka phones). Have all the participants bring a set of paper photo stencils and send them out to find corresponding shapes and colors that match the cards.

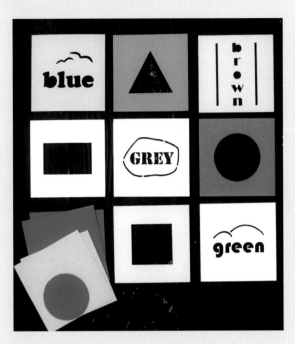

YOU'LL NEED

☐ Stencils (pages 176 and 177 or ones you come up with)
☐ Colored card stock
☐ Tape
☐ Cutting mat
☐ Utility knife, such as X-acto, or scissors
☐ Ruler
☐ Camera or phone

AT HOME

1. Create photo stencils. Photocopy or scan and print templates onto card stock or hand draw your own on 4¼-inch squares. On each of 8 cards, make your stencil, 4 with words: grey, green, blue, brown. And 4 with shapes: triangle, square, rectangle, circle.

2. Cut out the stencils. Securely tape the cards onto a cutting mat. Using a utility knife, cut out the shapes and letters.

ON THE TRAIL

3. Take photos. Give each participant a set of cards. While hiking, ask everyone to find corresponding colors and shapes to match each card (the cutout shapes can be used for extra credit). Hold up the card and take a photo of each discovery.

4. Have everyone share their photos for each card and give prizes for the best image in each category. Everyone wins!

Word Stencils

(enlarge 150%)

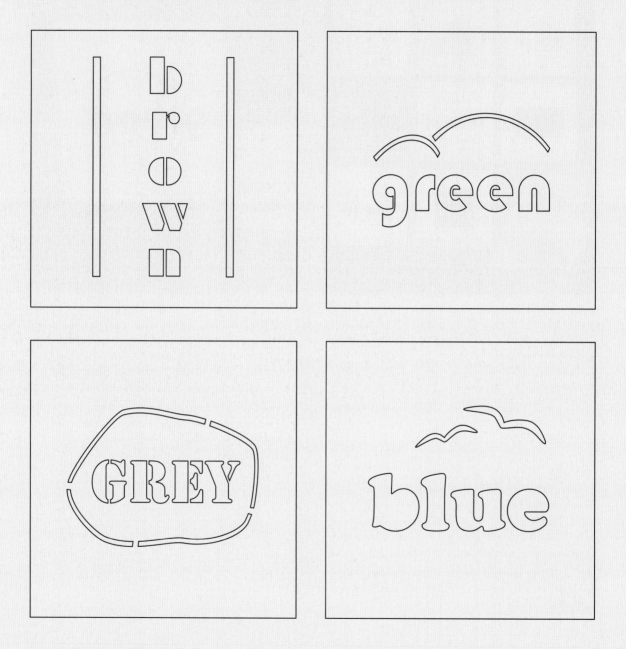

Shape Stencils
(enlarge 150%)

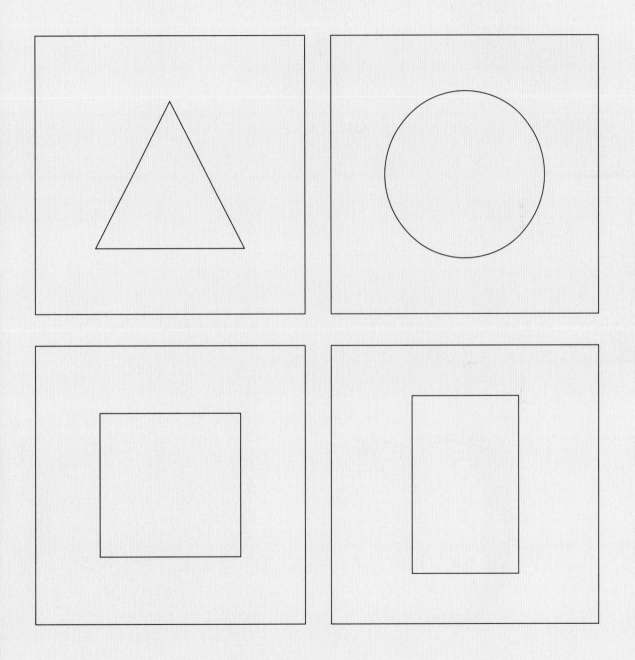

— Go —

FISH

The beautiful thing about fishing is that you can fail to catch even a minnow and still have a great time. Think about it: Fishing lets you settle in at a scenic spot on the shore of a lake or river, then do very little while waiting for that exhilarating moment when you feel a tug on the line—and spring into action. Sometimes nothing happens, but no matter. As master fly-tyer A. K. Best once said, "The fishing was good; it was the catching that was bad."

Fishing is a great activity when you're camping, and while the experts fish at a high level—focusing on the intricacies of gear and the eccentricities of individual fish species—it doesn't take much for beginners to get started. Here's a quick primer.

MANTI-LA SAL NATIONAL
FOREST, UTAH

— The —
BASICS

LICENSES

Rules about fishing licenses vary from state to state. Depending on where you plan to fish, you can pick up a short-term license, even a one-day license, online or from designated vendors. Lifetime licenses are also available. Age requirements vary, so check to see if your children will need their own licenses. A good source for information about rules in different states is *takemefishing.org*, which has a clickable map for each state.

WHERE TO GO

Check the state fish and wildlife department website for any restrictions at your planned location: Are there limits on catch—number, size, or species of fish—or on fishing method? Before casting your line in the water, spend some time observing. Fish hide from predators underneath logs, behind rocks, and in weeds, and they lie in wait for insects and other food. See if you can spot any fish; watch their behavior, and then cast your line.

CATCH AND RELEASE

Unless you plan to eat your catch (see "Bringing Your Catch Back to Camp," page 186), releasing a fish is the most eco-friendly thing to do. You also want to make sure that the fish is of legal size before you decide to keep it. For more efficient release, use a barbless hook or bend down the barbs on a hook with pliers so that they're less likely to catch in the fish's mouth. Wet your hands before handling a live fish, and try to keep the fish in the water as you ease the hook back through the lip (needlenose pliers are a helpful tool). Fish also often swallow the hook—if that happens, cut the line as close to the mouth as possible. If the fish isn't moving and appears to be in shock or dead, gently hold it facing the current to increase water flow to its gills. If you are lake or pond fishing, repeatedly move the fish through the water head-first to revive it.

— *Fishing* —
TACKLE

HOOKS

Simple as they are, you'll find that there are endless hook variations, depending on the kind of fish you're trying to catch and the bait you're using. Check at a sporting goods dealer or bait shop to figure out the proper hook for your needs. It's also easy enough to stock your tackle box with assorted sizes and shapes.

LINES

The size and strength of fishing lines are measured by pound-test, with the greater measurement indicating a stronger line. Bigger is not necessarily better if you are going after smaller fish that are unlikely to break a more modest line.

SINKERS

These weights help with casting, and bring and hold bait below the surface. Avoid sinkers made of lead, which harm water quality.

BOBBERS OR FLOATERS

You don't need anything fancy. Even tying a piece of cork with a stick in it to your line will do just fine. Traditional red-and-white plastic ball bobbers also work. You know you have a bite when the bobber suddenly begins moving up and down.

LIVE BAIT AND LURES

Beginners will generally be more successful with bait than with lures, and with lures than with fly-fishing. Minnows, worms, crayfish, and such insects as crickets and beetles are readily available and cheap to buy; if you don't want to bother digging for your own, any bait shop or sporting goods store with fishing gear will have what you need. Artificial lures require more technique but also work quite well, plus you eliminate the squirm factor of having to work with such critters as leeches. Another option is what's called dough balls, basically gunk (flour or cornmeal plus flavoring) prepared for certain fish species that you shape onto the hook.

NETS

Hooking a fish is one thing. Landing it is a whole other challenge. So you'll need a landing net. They vary in size, depending on the type of fish you're likely to catch, and come in a variety of materials. For catch-and-release, go for knotless rubber or coated nylon nets, which will be less damaging to the fish's scales. Black mesh material and handles will be less noticeable to fish, making the landing process easier. Net handles also vary in length and materials. Shorter handles made of lightweight aluminum are easier to use, although you will need to work the fish in more closely.

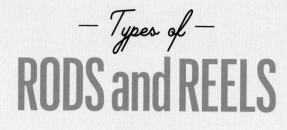

— Types of —
RODS and REELS

Especially if you're new to fishing, you'll probably want to rent before making the commitment to buy your own gear. You'll get a better idea of where you're likely to fish (and the species you're likely to fish for), as well as the kind of lure and bait you'll use.

CANE POLES

The easiest and cheapest way to try fishing, a cane pole is a simple rod with line and bobber tied to the end. Cane poles don't require casting skills (making them ideal for kids); simply bait the hook and drop the line where you wish.

SPIN-CASTING AND BAIT-CASTING

Maybe you have gotten hooked, so to speak, after playing around with a cane pole and want to try casting with something a little more advanced. A spin-casting outfit is an ideal next step. Spin-casting rods have a pistol-like grip with a reel and line guides sitting on top. Fiberglass spin-casting rods are a good choice because of their durability (another option is the more expensive graphite rods). Use spin-casting rods for panfish (smaller game fish that will fit into a frying pan), such as perch, bluegill, and crappie.

Spin-casting reels are easy for beginners to use, thanks to a button that controls the release of line as you cast. The reels are covered, so the line comes out of a small hole, thus reducing your chances of tangling the line. Spin-casting reels promote accuracy more than distance.

With either pistol grips or straight handles and reels mounted above the rod, bait-casting outfits are used with heavier bait and are good choices for such fish as bass, pike, and muskie. The reel is more complicated, with a line spool that turns when you cast, thus requiring more advanced technique to avoid snags.

SPINNING

Unlike spin-casting outfits, spinning gear features a rod with an open-face reel and line guides mounted on the bottom, not the top. The uncovered reel lets line out faster, allowing you to cast greater distances, but the gear takes more practice to master. Spinning rods and reels work well with lighter baits and lures.

FLY

Fly-fishing for trout or striped bass is fishing as art form, and there is no shortage of paeans to the sport. It's highly unlikely that you'll start with fly-fishing because of the advanced casting technique it requires. Weighted from 1 to 15, the long rods are flexible but strong and typically made of graphite or fiberglass. Mounted on the bottom of the rod, the elegant fly reel is designed to maximize fluid line action.

SALTWATER

More heavy-duty than freshwater gear, saltwater tackle is designed to catch larger fish and is often made of stainless steel to withstand the corrosive effects the ocean can have on such materials as aluminum.

BAIT-CASTING REEL

SPINNING REEL

CASTING

— 101 —

Spin-casting and spinning techniques are similar. The main difference is that the spin-casting reel has a push-button mechanism you use to release the line, while the spinning reel requires you to release line from the bail (the mechanism that controls the line) and hold it with your finger, before letting it out as you cast. The casting motion for both techniques is similar to throwing a baseball.

Spin-Casting

1. Hold the handle or grip and depress the thumb button on the reel.

2. While facing the target, turn your body at a slight angle with your rod arm toward the target.

3. With the rod aimed at the target, hold the rod tip at eye level.

4. In one motion, bend your casting arm from the elbow, bringing your hand to eye level.

5. When the rod begins bending, bring your forearm forward, and as the rod reaches eye level, release the thumb button.

Spinning

1. Hold the reel foot (the post attached to the rod) between your third and fourth fingers. Press the line between your index finger and the rod, then open the reel bail to release the line.

2. While facing the target, turn your body at a slight angle with your rod arm toward the target.

3. In one motion, bend your arm from the elbow, bringing your hand to eye level.

4. When the rod begins bending, bring your forearm forward, and as the rod reaches eye level, take your finger off the line to let it out.

Reel It In

After long stretches when nothing happens, the sudden pull on your line as a fish bites always gets the adrenaline flowing. The first thing you need to do is reel in the slack on your line, then set the hook with a short, quick lift of the rod. Once the hook is set, keep the rod up and use your reel to maintain tension on the line. If you notice the fish swimming away from you and heading into deeper water, hold your rod at a 45-degree angle toward the fish and let it run. Don't start reeling in line until the fish rests. Then lift your rod up to start bringing the fish in, before lowering the rod to create slack so you can reel in line. You might repeat this "pump and reel" sequence several times before the fish stops running and is close enough to land with a net. Hold the net in the water away from the fish to keep from spooking it, then ease it headfirst into the net before lifting up to pull the fish out of the water.

BRINGING YOUR

Catch Back to Camp

You caught one! *Now apply a quick, sharp blow to the top of its head with a hatchet handle or heavy stick to kill it instantly (the most humane way, according to the Washington Department of Fish and Wildlife). See "How to Clean a Fresh-Caught Fish" (page 133), and to cook your fresh catch, try our recipe for Trout with Browned Butter and Capers (page 133).*

SKAGIT RIVER,
WASHINGTON

— *Get* —

PADDLING

For many, canoes and kayaks evoke images of exploring the land of sky blue waters à la Lewis and Clark, and then finishing a long, hot day of paddling with an ice-cold beer in camp. For others, it conjures just one thing: the movie Deliverance. *Consider us part of the first group.*

MADELY LAKE, WHISTLER, BRITISH COLUMBIA

BEGINNERS' TIPS

LEARN FROM THE PROS. Find a good local outfitter with certified instructors who can give you a lesson, or try a guided journey before going it alone so you can get a feel for the experience without having to bear full responsibility.

PLAN A SHORT TRIP FIRST. You're trying to have fun, not find the Northwest Passage or claim new lands for the queen. Keep your ambitions in check.

MAP THE PUT-IN AND TAKE-OUT PROCESS. Depending on how many people are in your party, you will need at least two cars for a shuttle. It's common sense, but remember that the car (or cars) you leave at the take-out location needs to be able to transport the canoes or kayaks back to the put-in area where you left the first vehicle.

STAY CALM AND SKIP THE WHITEWATER. You'll face enough challenges without running the risk of capsizing in rapids. Stick to flatter water until you gain more experience. Always check river flow rates, because even a normally tranquil stream can become challenging during periods of high water. And low flows will mean additional portaging.

DON'T WEIGH YOURSELF DOWN. Canoes in particular can carry a lot of gear, much more than you could haul while hiking. But with additional loading and unloading of the boats, you'll regret overpacking.

USE SMALLER BAGS. Larger bags will give you fewer options for packing and weight distribution in the craft. Smaller bags also make it easier to form a human chain for easier loading and off-loading.

BE WATER-WISE. Put a change of clothes and spare pair of footwear in a bag separate from your other duds—in case your primary bag gets soaked. It also doesn't hurt to stash key items in a large plastic bag before stuffing it into a dry bag (see opposite page).

LEAVE YOUR ITINERARY WITH SOMEONE. Make sure a friend or relative knows your exact plans and can alert authorities if you haven't arrived or called by the anticipated time.

CANOE PADDLE
Single-bladed

KAYAK PADDLE
Two-bladed

— Basic—
GEAR

THE RIGHT CANOE When you go in and rent, let the salesperson know whether you'll be on a river or a lake and for how long. If you are going long distances, a touring canoe that can haul more gear may be a better choice than a general recreational one that is designed for day trips. Some touring canoes perform best on flat water, while others can handle rougher, faster currents. And longer canoes tend to be quicker and more efficient.

THE RIGHT KAYAK A sit-on-top kayak works perfectly well for short trips. It is lightweight, stable, and easy to get in and out of. For longer trips, get a touring kayak, which usually has a rudder for steering and offers storage space and sealed hatches.

PADDLES One of the biggest differences between kayaking and canoeing is the paddle. Kayaks use a two-bladed paddle, while canoes use single-bladed paddles. Get a paddle that fits your height and the size of the boat. And make sure you have extra paddles. Lose or break a paddle without having a spare and you will literally and figuratively be up a creek without one.

DRY BAGS Water is your friend; water is your enemy: Used properly, dry bags offer a way to transport clothing, sleeping bags, and other items you don't want to get wet. Made of such materials as coated nylon or vinyl, these top-loading, soft-sided sacks let you roll down the neck and force out any air, then close the opening and seal the bag tightly with a buckle so water can't enter. Some are transparent to allow you to see where everything is, while other dry bags have handles or harnesses, a nice plus if you anticipate a lot of portaging.

PERSONAL FLOTATION DEVICES (AKA LIFE JACKETS, AND THE LIKE) One for each person, even on calm lakes, with a couple of spares too.

QUICK-DRY CLOTHING, HATS, AND WATER SHOES OR STURDY SANDALS Plan to get wet, and dress accordingly.

— On the —
WATER

TIE DOWN AND SECURE YOUR GEAR. You don't want to lose anything overboard, and shifting, unbalanced gear will affect stability and make paddling less efficient. Canoes should sit flat in the water without either the front or back end lifting out of the water.

STAY ORGANIZED. You'll want to keep your gear below the gunwales (the top edges of a boat's sides) for better stability, with heavier items in the center along the bottom and lighter equipment at the ends to maintain maneuverability. The load should also be distributed equally from side to side.

HAVE ESSENTIALS SECURED WITHIN REACH. All maps and permits, as well as a compass, should be attached to you or nearby in a waterproof holder. Secure any extra paddles and place them within grabbing distance.

GOING TANDEM

Tandem paddling allows a family to paddle together, and two paddlers will get you to your destination faster.

TANDEM CANOE In a two-person canoe, the person in the back or stern should be the more experienced paddler. The rear paddler gets in first and gets out last. They steer while the person in the front or bow watches for obstacles and sets the pace. To begin paddling, the person in the front should paddle on one side of the canoe, while at the same time, the person in the back paddles on the opposite side of the canoe.

TANDEM KAYAK In a two-person kayak, the more experienced paddler should sit in the back as they control the steering. For best balance, the smaller person typically sits in the front. The front paddler should get into the kayak first. To begin paddling, decide which side of the boat you will start on; synchronize your paddling so the back paddler matches the stroke of the person in front.

BASIC
Paddling Terms

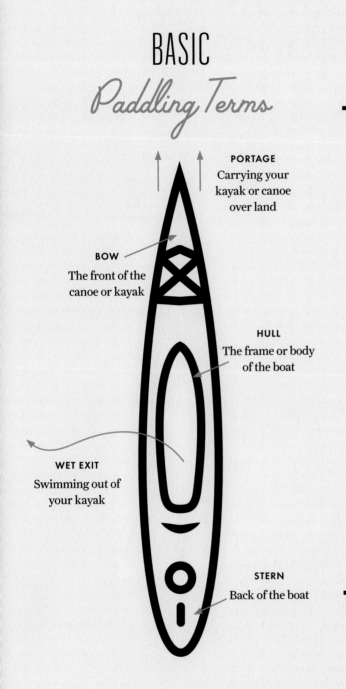

PORTAGE
Carrying your
kayak or canoe
over land

BOW
The front of the
canoe or kayak

HULL
The frame or body
of the boat

WET EXIT
Swimming out of
your kayak

STERN
Back of the boat

WHAT TO DO IF

You Capsize

In a kayak *Hold on to your paddle and kayak so they don't drift away. Flip the kayak upright. Reach for the opposite side of the kayak and pull yourself onto it. Swing your legs up and lie along the boat. Straddling the kayak with your legs in the water as you sit up will help with balance.*

In a canoe *Hold on to your paddle and canoe. If you are anywhere near shore, hang on to your boat and swim to shore before flipping the boat over. Otherwise, turn the boat completely upside down, tuck the paddles under the seat, and then duck under the boat into the air pocket under the boat. Get a firm grip on both sides at the center of the canoe, kick up to lift the boat, and flip it upright.*

CHAPTER 5

Fun IN CAMP

Just because you're not a kid anymore doesn't mean you can't enjoy a little playtime. After you've focused on your sleeping, eating, and hiking needs, REMEMBER TO PLAN FOR SOME SERIOUS FUN. Bring lyrics for sing-alongs, pack bingo cards, and reboot your creative side with nature-inspired crafts. Here are games, activities, and project ideas sure to keep everyone engaged and entertained for hours.

CAMP
— Sunset —
BINGO

Get your game on with these bingo cards. Making your own set will save you a few dollars, and these camping cards provide hours of pure old-school fun—they also do double duty for a woodsy wilderness scavenger hunt.

YOU'LL NEED
- ❑ Bingo card templates (pages 198 to 201)
- ❑ Card stock or heavyweight paper
- ❑ Clipboards (optional)
- ❑ Markers (at least 4 rocks, coins, etc., per player) or pencils

AT HOME
1. Photocopy or scan and print the templates onto card stock. Each player's card should be unique. Photocopy an extra card to use as the caller's card. Attach cards to clipboards if you like.

IN CAMP
2. Determine the rules: Decide the acceptable winning patterns (4 squares in a vertical, horizontal, or diagonal line; L-shape; or U-shape). Remember to come up with a prize for winning.
3. Hand out a bingo card and markers or a pencil to each player.
4. Play: Each player marks the Free Space. Caller calls out a square at random. When the square is called, each player marks it on their card with a rock marker or pencil. The first player to complete a winning pattern on their card calls out, *"Bingo!"*

Need to break a tie? Why not have a dance- or sing-off?

CAMP SUNSET BINGO

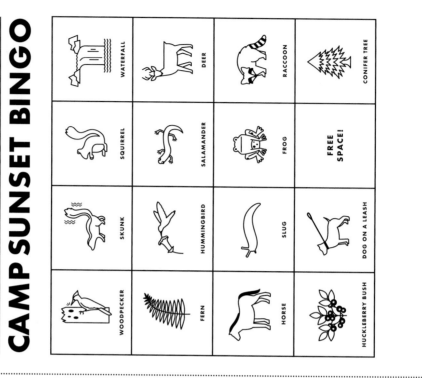

WATERFALL	SQUIRREL	SKUNK	WOODPECKER
DEER	SALAMANDER	HUMMINGBIRD	FERN
RACCOON	FROG	SLUG	HORSE
CONIFER TREE	FREE SPACE!	DOG ON A LEASH	HUCKLEBERRY BUSH

CAMP SUNSET BINGO

DOG ON A LEASH	RACCOON	HUMMINGBIRD	SALAMANDER
SQUIRREL	FERN	CONIFER TREE	WOODPECKER
SKUNK	DEER	WATERFALL	FROG
FREE SPACE!	HORSE	SLUG	HUCKLEBERRY BUSH

CAMP SUNSET BINGO

SKUNK	DOG ON A LEASH	WATERFALL	FROG
RACCOON	CONIFER TREE	FREE SPACE!	WOODPECKER
HUCKLEBERRY BUSH	DEER	HORSE	SQUIRREL
HUMMINGBIRD	FERN	SLUG	SALAMANDER

CAMP SUNSET BINGO

WOODPECKER	DOG ON A LEASH	WATERFALL	SKUNK
SLUG	HUCKLEBERRY BUSH	RACCOON	FREE SPACE!
FERN	FROG	CONIFER TREE	DEER
HORSE	SQUIRREL	SALAMANDER	HUMMINGBIRD

CAMP SUNSET BINGO

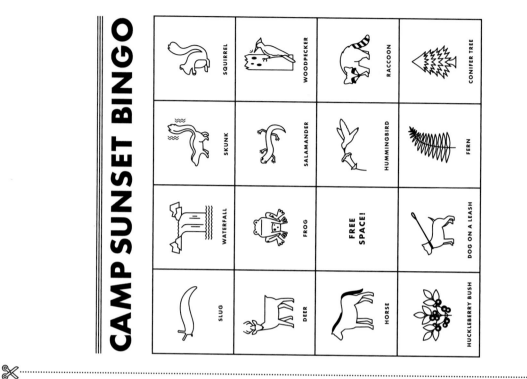

SQUIRREL	SKUNK	WATERFALL	SLUG
WOODPECKER	SALAMANDER	FROG	DEER
RACCOON	HUMMINGBIRD	FREE SPACE!	HORSE
CONIFER TREE	FERN	DOG ON A LEASH	HUCKLEBERRY BUSH

CAMP SUNSET BINGO

SLUG	RACCOON	HUMMINGBIRD	FREE SPACE!
SQUIRREL	HUCKLEBERRY BUSH	SKUNK	WOODPECKER
CONIFER TREE	DEER	WATERFALL	FROG
SALAMANDER	HORSE	DOG ON A LEASH	FERN

CAMP SUNSET BINGO

SKUNK	CONIFER TREE	SLUG	SALAMANDER
WOODPECKER	DOG ON A LEASH	DEER	FERN
FREE SPACE!	HUCKLEBERRY BUSH	HORSE	SQUIRREL
HUMMINGBIRD	RACCOON	WATERFALL	FROG

CAMP SUNSET BINGO

FROG	RACCOON	FERN	HORSE
CONIFER TREE	HUMMINGBIRD	DOG ON A LEASH	HUCKLEBERRY BUSH
WATERFALL	WOODPECKER	SLUG	DEER
SKUNK	SQUIRREL	SALAMANDER	FREE SPACE!

Tassel and Twig Necklace

This easy-to-make necklace of cotton cord and a simple twig can go from the campground straight to the city streets in style. Curl up by the fire and get knotty. These supplies are for one necklace, so don't forget to bring enough for everyone.

YOU'LL NEED

- ❏ Skein (at least 4 yards) of embroidery floss in any color, cut into one 7-foot piece and one 10-inch piece
- ❏ 2- to 2½-inch twig
- ❏ Scissors
- ❏ Skein of embroidery floss in a second color (optional)
- ❏ 41-inch length of 3mm cotton macramé cord

MAKE PENDANT

1. Create a loop: Wrap the 7-foot piece of embroidery floss around the ends of 4 fingers 25 to 30 times.

2. Insert twig and tie: Pull wrapped floss off fingers and slide the twig into one end of the loop. Tightly wrap the 10-inch piece of floss around the loop just under the twig. Tie a knot. Continue wrapping floss around the loop 3 or 4 more times and tie off with a double knot.

3. Make a tassel: Slide the blade of the scissors inside the loop. Pull tightly and cut to form the end of the tassel. Trim so that tassel ends are even.

Optional: Tie a 7-inch piece of floss in the second color around the wrapped knot area. Tie off and trim. This can add a bit of visual dynamics to the tassel.

ASSEMBLE NECKLACE

4. Fold macramé cord in half and set down. Place the pendant on the cord so twig is perpendicular to cord and 3 to 4 inches from the base of the cord loop. The tassel should be between the two strands of cord, with the loop just below the bottom of the tassel.

5. Fold the loop up 3 inches above twig. Pull the cut ends of the cord through the loop and pull tight to secure tassel. (The loop will be behind the two strands.)

6. To make an adjustable cord: Hold one strand of the cord 7 inches from the end. Wrap it three times around the opposite strand, wrapping toward the pendant. Pull the end back over the three wraps so it lies over them. Thread the end of the strand back under and through the wraps, toward the pendant. Hold the end of the strand above the wraps and pull to tighten and knot.

7. Repeat on other side. Adjust cord to desired length.

Optional: Finish the cord's ends with a 7-inch length of floss in the second color. Tie one end of the floss around a cord end, then lay the short floss end along the cord and wrap the rest of the floss around the cord, hiding the short end. Tie the floss in a double knot to secure. Repeat on other side.

Animal Masks

There's nothing more fun than playing make-believe, and having a mask makes pretending that much easier. Simple and playful paper masks help kids of all ages connect with their "wild" character.

YOU'LL NEED

☐ Animal mask templates (pages 206 to 209)
☐ Measuring tape or ruler
☐ Cutting mat (if using craft knife)
☐ Pencil
☐ Brown kraft paper (brown paper bags work well)
☐ Scissors or craft knife, such as X-acto
☐ Construction paper in various colors
☐ Quick-dry craft glue, such as Aleene's
☐ Fabric-covered elastic cord
☐ Mini stapler or hole punch
☐ Transparent tape

AT HOME

1. For each mask, measure the distance between the child's pupils. Photocopy or scan and print a template, enlarging it as necessary so the distance between the template's eyes matches that of your child's.

2. On the cutting mat, using the template, trace and cut the animal face out of kraft paper with scissors

or a craft knife. Cut out the eyeholes.

IN CAMP

3. Trace and cut out other mask features from construction paper in the color of your choice.

4. Use a thin layer of quick-dry glue to affix features onto the animal face. Allow to dry. (You can place the mask between two flat surfaces to help it dry flat.)

5. Cut a 15-inch length of elastic cord. Tie a knot at one end. Once mask is dry, staple one end of elastic cord to the back of mask, in line with the eyeholes. (You can also use a hole punch to make holes for the cord.) Place a piece of tape over the staple and knot for added security.

6. Place mask against your child's face and extend the cord around to other side of the mask, to determine length of the cord. Cut cord, leaving an extra 1/2 inch for a knot. Add a knot to the cut end, staple to the back of mask, and tape over the staple and knot.

Bear Mask Stencil

(enlarge 200%)

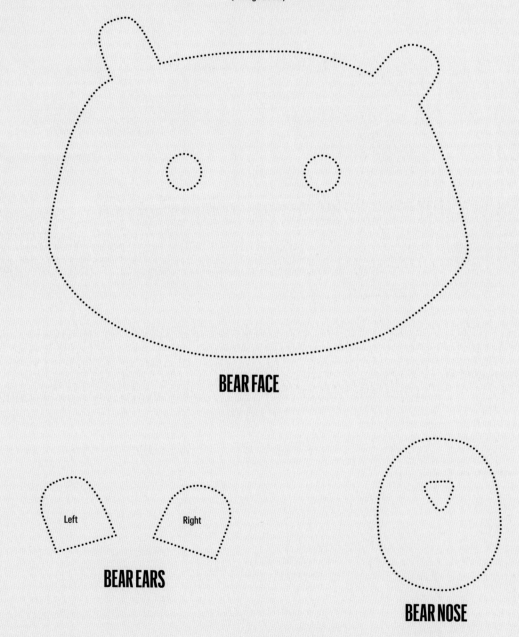

BEAR FACE

Left

Right

BEAR EARS

BEAR NOSE

Fox Mask Stencil

(enlarge 200%)

FOX FACE

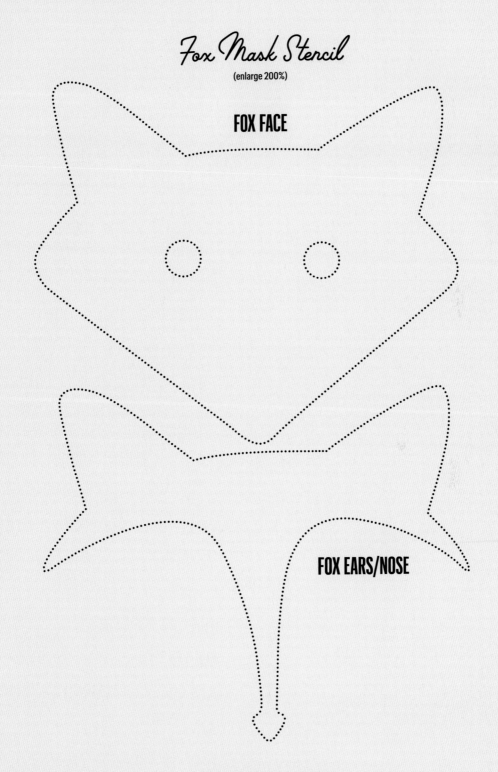

FOX EARS/NOSE

Owl Mask Stencil

(enlarge 200%)

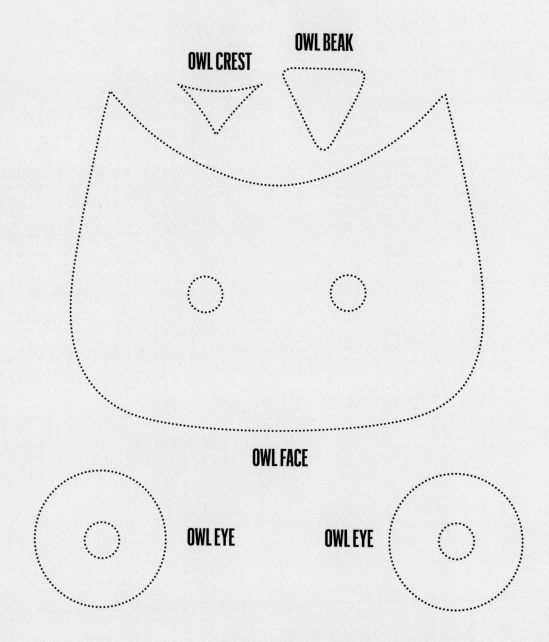

OWL CREST

OWL BEAK

OWL FACE

OWL EYE

OWL EYE

Raccoon Mask Stencil

(enlarge 200%)

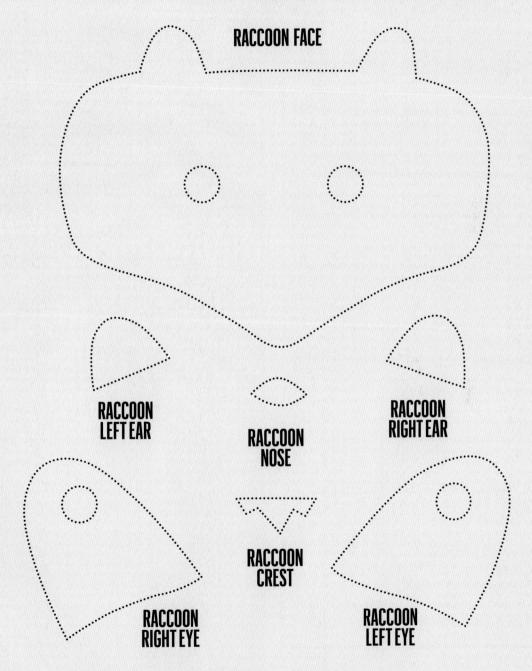

RACCOON FACE

RACCOON LEFT EAR

RACCOON NOSE

RACCOON RIGHT EAR

RACCOON RIGHT EYE

RACCOON CREST

RACCOON LEFT EYE

Sun-Print Notebooks

Harness the power of the sun to capture little moments of nature. Once created, these prints can be used to cover notebooks, journals, or sketchbooks that will become a beautiful and lasting reminder of your time spent camping in the great outdoors.

YOU'LL NEED

- ❑ One or two light-sensitive paper kits, such as Sunprint Kit, with 8- by 12-inch sheets*
- ❑ Piece of cardboard (at least 8 by 12 inches)
- ❑ Leaves, flowers, feathers, and other small natural items
- ❑ Plastic tub or container large enough to rinse the sheets (for water "developer")
- ❑ Paper towel
- ❑ Blank notebooks, large (about 7 by 10 inches) or small (about 4¾ by 7 inches)**
- ❑ Craft knife, such as X-acto, or scissors
- ❑ Ruler
- ❑ Cutting mat (if using craft knife)
- ❑ Pencil
- ❑ Permanent spray adhesive (for large notebooks)
- ❑ Double-sided transparent tape (for small notebooks)

IN CAMP

1. Read through your kit instructions for specific directions. In a shaded area, out of the direct sun, place the sun-print paper, treated side up, on a piece of cardboard. Arrange your objects on the paper until you get the composition desired. Place the acrylic pressing sheet on top to flatten the objects against sun-print paper.

2. Set the cardboard, sun-print paper, objects, and pressing sheet in direct sunlight. (If the objects shift,

NOTE BOOK
Most advanced quality
Gives best writing features

quickly replace.) Expose for 3 to 5 minutes, until the color disappears from the paper. When cloudy, the process may take longer. Create a variety of sun prints.

3. Fill the tub with water. After exposure, remove the objects and rinse your prints in the tub, 1 to 5 minutes, until the paper turns blue with white images. Lay your prints flat to dry on a paper towel or cardboard. (Once completely dry, you can flatten the prints under a book or board with a heavy weight—like a cast-iron skillet—on top, or smooth out wrinkles at home with an iron set on low.)

AT HOME

To cover large notebooks

1. Choose your favorite print and position it on the front of the notebook. Using a craft knife, ruler, and cutting mat, cut a clean edge along the print's left side, which will become the left edge of the cover (allow at least ⅝ inch of extra width).

2. Turn the sun print facedown on a protected work surface. Spray the back of the print with adhesive. Turn the print over and arrange it on the notebook, leaving a ½- to ⅝-inch margin on the left. Press the print down, working carefully from left to right to avoid trapping air bubbles.

3. Flip the notebook over, cover side down, on the cutting mat. Using the craft knife, carefully trim off any excess print along the edges of the notebook.

4. Repeat for the back of the notebook.

To cover small notebooks

1. Choose your favorite print and wrap it horizontally around the small notebook, positioning it so your favorite area is prominent. Pay extra attention to what you want on the front cover. Holding the print in place, lay it facedown, with the opened notebook, flat on a work surface.

2. Use a pencil to trace the top and bottom edges of the notebook on the back of the sun print. Cut the sun print to the exact height of your notebook.

3. Put the sun print facedown on the work surface and center the opened and flat notebook on it. Fold over the ends of the print and crease them along the edges of the notebook. Unfold, pull the notebook away, and fold the sun-print ends all the way down along the creased lines.

4. Use double-sided tape to adhere one flap of the sun print to the notebook, making sure the print lines up with top and bottom edges of the notebook. Repeat with the other flap.

*Sunprint Kits include coated paper that reacts to sunlight to create cyanotype prints (like a blueprint); find kits at science or children's museum stores, or at sunprints.org. Other cyanotype kits are made by SunArt Paper (tedco toys.com) and NaturePrint (natureprintpaper.com).
**Dark notebook covers with little or no contrasting pattern or text are best, as light colors and high-contrast printing will show through the sun print.

Blue Admiral

Speckled Skipper

Blue Heather

Common Pinky

Spotted Emperor

Leaf Butterflies

Use acrylic paint to transform one natural wonder into another. Paint dots, stripes, and squiggles on matching sets of leaves and create a kaleidoscope of wings. Commemorate your trip by displaying the brand-new species of butterfly.

YOU'LL NEED

❑ A collection of leaves (dried leaves work best)
❑ Acrylic paints
❑ Paintbrushes
❑ Clear acrylic spray sealer (or for a more kid-friendly option, use white craft glue diluted with an equal amount of water)
❑ Foam-core board or cardboard for mounting
❑ Straight pins

OPTIONAL ROPE BORDER AND LABELS

❑ Quick-dry craft glue, such as Aleene's
❑ Rope
❑ Pen and paper
❑ Scissors
❑ Double-stick transparent tape

1. Remove stems from leaves.

2. Match smaller leaves into pairs; each leaf will be a wing. Large leaves can be butterflies on their own.

3. On a protected work surface, and using acrylics, paint the leaves with designs of dots, stripes, and geometric shapes. Let paint dry.

4. Seal and preserve the leaves with the acrylic spray sealer or diluted glue. Give them a thorough coat, making sure to include the edges. (Follow the manufacturer's safety instructions on the spray.) Allow the leaves to dry.

5. Place the leaves in butterfly shapes on the foam core. Use pins to secure the leaves by sticking pins gently through the ends of leaves and into foam core.

Optional: Glue a rope border around the board. Make up a faux scientific name for each butterfly and add a label underneath using double-stick tape.

HOW TO

Merit Badges

Whether you're 6 or 60-something, you can appreciate the spirit of challenge—okay, and competition—
in earning accolades for your mad camping skills. Photocopy or scan and print these badges onto sticker
paper or turn them into pin-back buttons using a button-making kit. Then let the fun begin!

Get ready to go
PAGE 44

Pack a cooler
PAGE 46

Set up camp
PAGE 55

Learn about nature
PAGE 168

Build a campfire
PAGE 66

Make camp cocktails
PAGE 108

Serve a fancy dinner
PAGE 117

Wash dishes in camp
PAGE 83

Sing around the campfire
PAGE 220

Brew coffee like a barista
PAGE 97

Cook breakfast
PAGE 86

Make camp crafts
PAGE 202

Take a nap in nature
PAGE 37

Kids help cook
PAGE 84

Cook in a dutch oven
PAGE 112

Make s'mores
PAGE 148

Tell a spooky story
PAGE 222

Leave no trace
PAGE 74

Wood and flame make a campfire burn, but the songs we sing around it are what give it warmth. Your roommate with the never-been-tuned ukulele or the uncle who "strums a little guitar" but still, after 23 years, hasn't budged from the second verse of "Brown Eyed Girl": They're the heroes of the campfire. Without them, the hours between s'mores and snores would be fast and forgetful.

Start with a traditional song, like "Bill Grogan's Goat," which has some call-and-response in it. Everyone can participate: You don't have to sing in tune or play an instrument or even know the words. Hum, clap, bang on a log, as long as you're part of the process.

We've included quite a few selections from campfire's greatest hits, including "Kumbaya" and "You Are My Sunshine," but depending on the group, give some of these other universal favorites a try. Start with traditional or children's songs and move on to modern pop songs. If you're looking for a good book with lyrics and guitar chords for the classic numbers, we like *Rise Up Singing: The Group Singing Songbook* by Peter Blood and Annie Patterson (Hal Leonard, 2005).

THE TOP
150 Campfire Songs

Broadway

Do-Re-Mi; Edelweiss; Food, Glorious Food; Getting to Know You; If Ever I Would Leave You; If I Were a Rich Man; My Favorite Things; Oh, What a Beautiful Mornin'; Oklahoma; Seventy-Six Trombones; Some Enchanted Evening; The Sound of Music; Summer Nights; Sunrise, Sunset

Patriotic

America the Beautiful; God Bless America; Home on the Range; Roll On, Columbia; This Land Is Your Land

Children's Songs

Baby Beluga; B-I-N-G-O; Down by the Bay; The Eensy Weensy Spider; Going to the Zoo; I Am a Pizza; If You're Happy and You Know It; I Know an Old Lady; I'm a Little Teapot; Let It Go; Oats, Peas, Beans, and Barley Grow; Old MacDonald Had a Farm; On Top of Spaghetti; Sarasponda; This Old Man

Folk Songs

Blowin' in the Wind; The Bramble and the Rose; Day by Day; Five Hundred Miles; The Fox; Hobo's Lullaby; Go Down, Moses; If I Had a Hammer; I Shall Be Released; Joe Hill; Michael Row the Boat Ashore; On Top of Old Smokey; Shenandoah; Shortnin' Bread; Take Me Home, Country Roads; Turn! Turn! Turn!; The Wabash Cannonball; Where Have All the Flowers Gone?

The Beatles

Blackbird; Here Comes the Sun; Hey Jude; Imagine; Let It Be; Nowhere Man; Ob-La-Di, Ob-La-Da; Octopus's Garden; Penny Lane; We Can Work It Out; When I'm Sixty-Four; With a Little Help from My Friends; Yellow Submarine; Yesterday

Pop/Rock (Classic)

American Pie; Brown Eyed Girl; Desperado; Downtown; Fire and Rain; Heart of Gold; Homeward Bound; House of the Rising Sun; I Can See Clearly Now; I Heard It Through the Grapevine; Jack & Diane; King of the Road; Lean on Me; Margaritaville; Moonshadow; Morning Has Broken; My Generation; My Girl; Proud Mary; Raindrops Keep Fallin' on My Head; Ripple; Rivers of Babylon; Rocket Man; Rocky Mountain High; Scarborough Fair; Shower the People; Sitting on the Dock of the Bay; Stand By Me; Sweet Home Alabama; Teach Your Children; Tracks of My Tears; What the World Needs Now Is Love; Will You Love Me Tomorrow; You've Got a Friend

Pop/Rock (Modern)

Call Me Maybe; Chasing Cars; Drops of Jupiter; FourFiveSeconds; Good Riddance (Time of Your Life); Happy; Hey, Soul Sister; Hey There Delilah; I'm Yours; Love Story; Photograph; Riptide; Thinking Out Loud; 22; Wagon Wheel; Waiting on the World to Change; We Are Young; When I Was Your Man; Wonderwall

Traditional

Amazing Grace; Bill Grogan's Goat; Clementine; Cockles and Mussels; Comin' Thro' the Rye; Danny Boy; Down by the Old Mill Stream; Down by the Salley Gardens; Down in the Valley; Drunken Sailor; The Erie Canal; Hush, Li'l Baby; I've Been Working on the Railroad; John Jacob Jingleheimer Schmidt; Kumbaya; Lavender's Blue; Make New Friends; Polly Wolly Doodle; Red Is the Rose; Red River Valley; The Riddle Song; She'll Be Comin' 'Round the Mountain; Skip to My Lou; Streets of Laredo; Take Me Out to the Ballgame; Waltzing Matilda; When Irish Eyes Are Smiling; Wild Mountain Thyme; Wild Rover; Wraggle-Taggle Gypsies; You Are My Sunshine

— *How to Tell a Terrific* —
CAMPFIRE STORY

In the outdoors, you depend on one another for entertainment. You bring a lot of gear, and you bring stories too. Enjoy this unplugged time, when everybody gets to be the audience, and the star. The following topics almost always spark good campfire stories.

YOUR NAME Hate it? Love it? How did you get it?

FOOD The food you most love, the food you most hate—and why you hate it.

ANIMAL ENCOUNTERS You and a bear/snake/moose/raccoon.

WILDERNESS TALES Something that happened while camping.

MUSIC MEMORY A piece of music that has meant something special.

FAVORITE PLACES A spot you used to love to go to. Think about all the sensory details. Remember the approach to the place.

HOW TO TELL A SPOOKY CAMPFIRE STORY

Wait until night falls and it is especially dark and creepy. Call for silence before you begin. Your audience will be carefully listening to the strange nighttime noises around them. Act out the story with your whole body and voice. Build suspense and let the story unfold slowly. Go into extra detail to engage their imagination. And end with a surprise or twist. Here are other elements to creating a spine-tingling tale.

Give your story a good setting
Think nighttime, a full moon, haunted places, the woods, or somewhere near where you are camping.

Add a terrifying element
Think about what scares you, whether it is monsters, murderous clowns, or being confined in a small space, and add it as a component in your story.

Truth or fiction?
Draw on an urban legend or base your story on true events to give it a ring of authenticity and keep listeners guessing.

STARGAZING

Camping gives you a chance to see the star-studded sky as our ancestors once did, especially in parks that have earned a designation as an International Dark Sky Park (see list, page 227). Maximize your constellation viewing with these tips.

Limit the use of lighting around your campsite
Use only illumination that is fully shielded and directs light down. Shine flashlights and headlamps toward the ground.

Let your eyes adjust
It takes from 20 to 30 minutes for your eyes to adapt to the darkness and see the night sky more fully. A good test is whether you can view each of the stars in the Little Dipper.

Keep current on planetary happenings
Check websites like *stardate.org* for updates on any celestial events taking place while you're camping. A full moon will wash out a big swath of the sky. New or crescent moons are ideal; or check for nights when the moon rises late or sets early.

Find an open area
You want to take in as expansive a sweep of the sky as possible.

Go out in fall or winter
Granted, it will get chilly, but the low humidity makes for crisper skies.

Go out with a ranger
Many national and state parks conduct stargazing events.

VIEWING MILKY WAY FROM
NATURAL BRIDGES NATIONAL
MONUMENT, UTAH

GEAR

WIDE-ANGLE BINOCULARS You don't need an expensive telescope to enhance your view of the night sky. A pair of 10x50 binoculars will make a huge difference. Or pick up a pair of astronomy binoculars with a mount for a tripod.

STAR CHART You can use an old-school chart like the glow-in-the-dark poster included with this book, or download one of the many apps for smartphones or tablets that make it easy for amateurs to accurately identify what's in the sky from their precise location.

COMPASS It can help you stay oriented as you look across the sky.

FLASHLIGHT WITH A RED BEAM The red light will have a less disruptive effect once everyone's eyes have adjusted to the dark. For a quick, cheap red filter, use red-colored plastic or paper to cover the end of a regular flashlight.

RECLINING CHAIR No, not a Barcalounger. But if you have a camp chair or cot, you'll save yourself neck strain.

HOW TO FIND THE DIPPERS AND POLARIS (THE NORTH STAR)

Although most people consider it the best-known and easiest-to-find constellation, technically the Big Dipper is not one of the 88 defined constellations. Instead, it's what's known as an asterism, a group of stars forming a pattern that's often part of a larger constellation. The Big Dipper is part of the tail and rear flank of the constellation Ursa Major (the Great Bear).

That said, the Big Dipper is one of the easiest astronomical patterns to identify and can help lead to other features in the sky. To find the Big Dipper, go to a spot with a clear view of the northern sky and horizon. During spring and summer, the Big Dipper will hang higher in the sky, while in fall and winter, you should search closer to the horizon.

Once you've located it (the formation may be on an angle), take note of Merak and Dubhe, the two stars that form the edge of the bowl away from the handle. They're nicknamed the Pointers, and Dubhe is the higher of the two. If you extend the imaginary line Dubhe creates with Merak, it leads to Polaris (aka the North Star). Polaris is the star at the tip of the Little

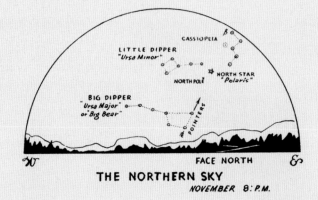

THE NORTHERN SKY
NOVEMBER 8: P.M.

Dipper's handle, which requires darker skies to see clearly because four of its stars are somewhat dim. And keep in mind that despite popular belief, Polaris is prominent but not the brightest star in the sky.

DARK-SKY PARKS

The International Dark-Sky Association has honored a number of parks around the world for their exceptional night skies and efforts to minimize light pollution that can obscure the stars. Here's a list of dark-sky parks in North America that offer camping:

ARIZONA Grand Canyon–Parashant National Monument

CALIFORNIA Anza-Borrego Desert State Park (surrounding the Dark Sky community of Borrego Springs), Death Valley National Park

COLORADO Black Canyon of the Gunnison National Park

FLORIDA Kissimmee Prairie Preserve State Park

NEW MEXICO Chaco Culture National Historical Park, Clayton Lake State Park

PENNSYLVANIA Cherry Springs State Park

TENNESSEE Pickett State Park

TEXAS Big Bend National Park, Copper Breaks State Park, Enchanted Rock State Natural Area

UTAH Canyonlands National Park, Capitol Reef National Park, Hovenweep National Monument, Natural Bridges National Monument, Weber County North Fork Park

VIRGINIA Staunton River State Park

— Resource Guide —

Here's where to discover campgrounds, make a reservation,
and find gear and supplies to help you plan your next camping trip.

CAMPGROUNDS

Hipcamp.com
Online guide to public land campsites as well as sites on ranches, farms, vineyards, and land preserves

Kampgrounds of America
koa.com
Network of established camp-grounds with amenities

National Park Service
nps.gov
Learn about 400 sites across America by state and by park; discover history; explore nature

Recreation.gov
Booking site for campgrounds in national parks, national forests, and other federal lands

ReserveAmerica.com
The biggest campground reservation system

FISHING

Takemefishing.org
Extensive fishing and boating resource, including fish species by region; how to fish; gear; boating basics; fishing rules by state; and water safety

GEAR

Amazon.com
Online retailer of gear, clothing, and provisions

Backcountry.com
Online retailer of gear and clothing

Bass Pro Shops
basspro.com
Gear for camping, fishing, and boating

Cabela's
cabelas.com
Gear for camping, fishing, and boating

Campmor
Campmor.com
Clothing, footwear, and gear

CampSaver
Campsaver.com
Online retailer of gear and clothing

Coleman
coleman.com
Wide range of gear, includ-ing coolers, lighting, nesting all-in-one portable sink for dishwashing, stoves such as models with HyperFlame built-in windscreens

Dick's Sporting Goods
Dickssportinggoods.com
Wide range of clothing and gear

Eastern Mountain Sports
ems.com
Wide range of clothing and gear

GetOutfitted
getoutfitted.com
Online rental of gear and clothing

L.L. Bean
llbean.com
Clothing and gear

Moosejaw Mountaineering
moosejaw.com
Clothing and gear

Mountain Equipment Co-op
Mec.ca
Canadian retailer of clothing and gear

Organize.com
Picnic and storage baskets (with handles) by Iris

Patagonia
patagonia.com
Wide range of clothing, gear, and provisions

REI
rei.com
Wide range of clothing and gear, including coolers; lighting; stoves, such as Primus FireHole 100 and 200; collapsible canteen; and more

Sierra Trading Post
Sierratradingpost.com
Clothing and gear

Stansport
stansport.com
Wide range of camping gear, including folding, heavy-duty camp grill grates

Wal-mart
Walmart.com
Wide range of gear and supplies

STARGAZING

SkySafari
Stargazing app

SkyView
Stargazing app

Stardate.org
Wide range of stargazing resources, including constella-tions, current celestial events, and much more

Star Walk
Stargazing app

COOKING EQUIPMENT

Arctic Ice
arctic-ice.com
Reusable cooler packs, including oversized ones to freeze for coolers

Crow Canyon Home
crowcanyonhome.com
Enamel tableware

Lodge
lodgemfg.com
Cast-iron skillets and camp dutch ovens

Nalgene
nalgene.com
Reusable BPA-free plastic bottles and containers, including oversized ones to freeze for coolers

Weber
weber.com
Charcoal chimneys and grilling gloves, grates, and tongs

CRAFT SUPPLIES

A.C. Moore Arts and Crafts
acmoore.com
General craft supplies

Hobby Lobby
hobbylobby.com
General craft supplies

Jo-Ann Fabric and Craft Store
joann.com
General craft supplies, including embroidery floss and cords

Michael's
michaels.com
General craft supplies

NaturePrint
natureprintpaper.com
Light-sensitive paper kits

Staples
staples.com
General supplies, including a selection of cardstock and papers

SunArt Paper
tedcotoys.com
Light-sensitive paper kits

Sunprint
sunprints.org
Light-sensitive paper kits

NATURE GUIDES

Audubon Wildflowers App
Flower identification app

Audubon's Field Guide to North American Trees
Tree identification app

Leafsnap
Plant identification app

NatureGate
Plant and wildlife identification app

ORGANIZATIONS

Leave No Trace Center for Outdoor Ethics
lnt.org

Outdoor Afro
outdoorafro.com

Sierra Club
Sierraclub.org

— Measurement Equivalents —

Refer to the following charts for metric conversions as well as common cooking equivalents. All equivalents are approximate.

Length

⅛ in.	=				3 mm.		
¼ in.	=				6 mm.		
½ in.	=				13 mm.		
¾ in.	=				2 cm.		
⅞ in.	=				2.2 cm.		
1 in.	=				2.5 cm.		
1½ in.	=				3.8 cm.		
2 in.	=				5 cm.		
2½ in.	=				6.5 cm.		
3 in.	=				7.5 cm.		
4 in.	=				10 cm.		
5 in.	=				12.5 cm.		
6 in.	=	½ ft.	=		15 cm.		
7 in.	=				18 cm.		
8 in.	=				20.5 cm.		
9 in.	=				23 cm.		
10 in.	=				25.5 cm.		
11 in.	=				28 cm.		
12 in.	=	1 ft.	=		30.5 cm.		
24 in.	=	2 ft.	=		61 cm.		
36 in.	=	3 ft.	=	1 yd.	=	91 cm.	
40 in.	=	3⅓ ft.			101.5 cm.	=	1 m.
41 in.	=				104 cm.		
84 in.	=	7 ft.	=		213 cm.	=	2.1 m.
144 in.	=	12 ft.	=	4 yd	=	366 cm.	=	3.7 m.

Cooking/Oven Temperatures

	FAHRENHEIT	CELSIUS	GAS MARK
Freeze Water	32°F	0°C	
Room Temp.	68°F	20°C	
Boil Water	212°F	100°C	
Bake	325°F	160°C	3
	350°F	180°C	4
	375°F	190°C	5
	400°F	200°C	6
	425°F	220°C	7
	450°F	230°C	8
Broil			Grill

Liquid Ingredients by Volume

¼ tsp.	=					1 ml.	
½ tsp.	=					2 ml.	
1 tsp.	=					5 ml.	
3 tsp.	=	1 tbsp.	=	½ fl. oz.	=	15 ml.	
2 tbsp.	=	⅛ cup	=	1 fl. oz.	=	30 ml.	
4 tbsp.	=	¼ cup	=	2 fl. oz.	=	60 ml.	
5⅓ tbsp.	=	⅓ cup	=	3 fl. oz.	=	80 ml.	
8 tbsp.	=	½ cup	=	4 fl. oz.	=	120 ml.	
10⅔ tbsp.	=	⅔ cup	=	5 fl. oz.	=	160 ml.	
12 tbsp.	=	¾ cup	=	6 fl. oz.	=	180 ml.	
16 tbsp.	=	1 cup	=	8 fl. oz	=	240 ml.	
1 pt.	=	2 cups	=	16 fl. oz.	=	480 ml.	
1 qt.	=	4 cups	=	32 fl. oz.	=	960 ml.	
				33 fl. oz.	=	1,000 ml.	=	1 l.

Dry Ingredients by Weight

1 oz.	=	1/16 lb.	=	30 g.
4 oz.	=	1/4 lb.	=	120 g.
8 oz.	=	1/2 lb.	=	240 g.
12 oz.	=	3/4 lb.	=	360 g.
16 oz.	=	1 lb.	=	480 g.

(To convert ounces to grams, multiply the number of ounces by 30.)

Equivalents for Different Types of Ingredients

STANDARD CUP	FINE POWDER (E.G., FLOUR)	GRAIN (E.G., RICE)	GRANULAR (E.G., SUGAR)	LIQUID SOLIDS (E.G., BUTTER)	LIQUID (E.G., MILK)
1	140 g.	150 g.	190 g.	200 g.	240 ml.
3/4	105 g.	113 g.	143 g.	150 g.	180 ml.
2/3	93 g.	100 g.	125 g.	133 g.	160 ml.
1/2	70 g.	75 g.	95 g.	100 g.	120 ml.
1/3	47 g.	50 g.	63 g.	67 g.	80 ml.
1/4	35 g.	38 g.	48 g.	50 g.	60 ml.
1/8	18 g.	19 g.	24 g.	25 g.	30 ml.

— Acknowledgments —

THIS BOOK WOULD NOT HAVE BEEN POSSIBLE WITHOUT the talent and passion of the team behind the original Camp Sunset, a weekend adventure where the editors of *Sunset* magazine took two families camping in the redwoods. From *Sunset*, thanks to Bruce Anderson, Peter Fish, Maili Holiman, Elaine Johnson (who also guided the overall vision of this book), Supriya Kalidas, Megan McCrea, Andrea Minarcek, Nino Padova, Sara Schneider, Yvonne Stender, Thomas J. Story, and Ebbe Roe Yovino-Smith. A big shout-out to our intrepid families, Tami Codianne-Miller and Riley and Scott Miller; and Ann-Marie, Ella, Greg, and Maya Torres. Thanks go as well to our guest experts, storyteller Joel ben Izzy; fire-builder and Alameda County, California, fireman Charohn Dawson and his son Malcolm Dawson; musicians Ben and Alex Morrison of The Brothers Comatose and Philip Brezina; Roland Mott and Danielle Rowland from Subaru/Leave No Trace Traveling Trainers Program; and ranger Alex Tabone of Big Basin Redwoods State Park. From previous *Sunset* stories, our thanks go to additional campers shown in this book, including Outdoor Afro founder Rue Mapp and her family Sherrita Cole, Arwen Kreber-Mapp, Seth Kreber-Mapp, Samara Cole Mercado, and Delane Sims; plus Clay Anderson; Tammy Nerwin and Luke Panezich; and Sara Paloma and Clara and Miles Story.

Special thank-you to writer Matt Jaffe for providing the perfect blend of expertise and humor for the book, organizing our words of wisdom, and adding greatly to the content on getting ready, basic skills, and outdoor exploration. To artist and writer Paige Russell, a big thank-you for creating the book's charming and very doable craft projects.

For contributing to our camping recipes, kudos to *Sunset* food editor Margo True and test kitchen manager Angela Brassinga; food writers April Cooper, Amy Machnak, Stephanie Spencer, Adeena Sussman, Kate Washington, and Molly Watson; plus the *Sunset* recipe testers—Kevyn Allard, Kay Bates, Sarah Epstein, Lenore Grant, Melissa Kaiser, Marlene Kawahata, Rebecca Parker, and Maryanne Welton.

We would also like to thank Gina Goff, José Guzman, Emma Star Jensen, Peggy Northrop, and Alan Phinney.

LAKE CHELAN,
WASHINGTON

— Index —

RED ROCK CANYON NATIONAL
CONSERVATION AREA, NEVADA

turkey black bean chili, 98
vegetables,
   ember-roasted, 130
Photography, 171
Photo safari, 174–77
Pistachio butter, rib-eye steak
  with asparagus and, 118
Pizza
  camp, with sausage and
    fontina, 130
  customizing, 130
  scrambled eggs, 90
Plants, identifying, 168–69
Poison oak, ivy, and
  sumac, 73
Polaris, 227
Potatoes
  hobo bundles, 125
  skewers, grilled onion,
    bacon, and, 137
  skillet breakfast, 90
Power sources, 36

Q, R

Quinoa, red, kale salad
  with carrots and, 138
Raccoons
  mask, 209
  safety and, 70
Rain fly, 18, 28, 29, 60, 61
Ranch dressing,
  homemade, 126
Raspberry cake, 143
Recycling, 64
Red Rock Canyon National
  Conservation Area,
  Nevada, 239
Reservations, 25
Rice, paella-style chicken
  and, 122
Rolls
  cheddar cheese, 94
  cinnamon, easy dutch
    oven, 94
RVs, 22

S

Salads
  hands-on, 137
  kale, with red quinoa and
    carrots, 138
  spinach and orzo, 134
Salmon packets, grilled, 126
Samuel P. Taylor State Park,
  California, 10
Sand
  managing, 18
  stakes, 17
Sandwiches
  egg salad, with herb
    mayo, 101

hot dogs, cowboy, 101
vegetable, grilled
  Mediterranean, 121
Sangria, camp cooler, 109
Sausage
  and bean dutch oven
    stew, 118
  camp pizza with fontina
    and, 130
  hobo bundles, Italian-
    style, 125
  hot dogs, cowboy, 101
  pizza scrambled eggs, 90
Saws, 35
Sawtooth National Recreation
  Area, Idaho, 2
Scavenger hunt, 174–77
Scorpions, 17
Sea beans, 103
Sesame seeds
  date bars, 104
  granola, almond, cherry,
    and, 93
Shade, 15, 18, 36
Shakshouka, breakfast, 89
Sheep marshmallow
  animal, 152
Shoes, 158
Shovels, 35
Showers, 36
Shrimp
  chicken and rice,
    paella-style, 122
Sinkers, 182
Sinks, portable, 43
Skagit River, Washington, 187
Skills
  building a campfire, 66–67
  cleaning fish, 133
  identifying plants and trees,
    168–69
  packing a cooler, 46
  photograph like a pro, 171
  stargazing, 225, 227
  telling campfire stories, 222
  tent, setting up, 58–60
  tying knots, 62–63
Sleeping
  bags, 30–31, 75
  other gear for, 32
  pads, 32, 75
S'mores, 148–49
  trail mix, 107
Snake River, Jackson Hole,
  Wyoming, 178–179
Snakes, 17, 72
Songs, 220–21
Soup, curried coconut
  lentil, 114
Spinach
  and orzo salad, 134
  skillet breakfast potatoes, 90
Spruce tips, 103
Stakes, 17, 29, 60

Stargazing, 225, 227
Steaks
  New York, pan-seared, and
    mushrooms, 117
  rib-eye, with pistachio butter
    and asparagus, 118
Stinging nettles, 73
Stories, campfire, 222
Stoves, 40, 80
Streams, crossing, 166

T

Tassel and twig necklace,
  202–3
Taut-line hitch, 63
Tents
  construction of, 28–29
  features of, 29
  location of, 57
  packing, 75
  pitching, 57, 58–60
  shopping for, 28
  size of, 28
  tips for, 61
  types of, 27
  weather and, 28
Tequila
  cinnamon tea with, 109
  margarita, 109
Ticks, 72
Tides, 18
Timothy Lake, Oregon, 55
Toiletries, 50
Tomatoes
  chicken and rice, paella-
    style, 122
  chicken enchilada nacho
    bowls, 98
  hands-on salad, 137
  huevos rancheros con
    bacon, 89
  kebabs, cool, 110
  lentil soup, curried
    coconut, 114
  penne all'amatriciana, 129
  pizza scrambled eggs, 90
  sandwiches, grilled
    Mediterranean
    vegetable, 121
  shakshouka, breakfast, 89
  spinach and orzo
    salad, 134
  turkey black bean chili, 98
Tools, 35
Tortilla chips
  chicken enchilada nacho
    bowls, 98
Tortillas
  huevos rancheros con
    bacon, 89
  warming, 89
Trailers, 22, 23

Trail mix
  monkey business, 107
  s'mores, 107
Trash, 64, 74
Trees
  dead, 54
  identifying, 168–69
Trout with browned butter
  and capers, 133
Trowels, 35
Turkey
  black bean chili, 98
  hobo bundles, Italian-
    style, 125

V

Vegetables. See also
  individual vegetables
  ember-roasted, 138
  pizza, veggie camp, 130
  sandwiches, grilled
    Mediterranean, 121
Vermouth
  negronis, 109

W–Z

Wasps, 72
Water
  carrier, 43
  importance of, 17
  sources, 54, 74
Whipped cream, 144
Wildlife
  feeding, 74
  photographing, 171
  respecting, 74
  safety, 17, 54, 70, 74,
    164–65
Wind, 17, 40, 60
Wine
  sangria, camp cooler, 109
Wonder Lake Campground,
  Denali National Park,
  Alaska, 76–77
Yellow jackets, 72
Yosemite National Park
  Dewey Point, 170–171
  Tuolumne Meadows, 12
  Yosemite Valley, 172–173
Zaatar and lemon grilled
  chicken, 121
Zucchini
  pizza, veggie camp, 130
  sandwiches, grilled
    Mediterranean
    vegetable, 121